Paul Quarrington

FROM THE FAR SIDE OF THE RIVER

Chest-Deep in Little Fish and Big Ideas

GREY*S*TONE BOOKS

Douglas & McIntyre Publishing Group
Vancouver/Toronto/New York

Copyright © 2003 by Paul Quarrington

03 04 05 06 07   5 4 3 2 1

Greystone Books
A division of Douglas & McIntyre Ltd.
2323 Quebec Street, Suite 201
Vancouver, British Columbia
Canada V5T 4S7
www.greystonebooks.com

National Library of Canada Cataloguing in Publication Data

Quarrington, Paul
  From the far side of the river: chest-deep in little fish and big ideas/Paul Quarrington

  ISBN 1-55054-979-0

  1. Fishing—Anecdotes. I. Title.
PS8583.U334F76 2003   C818/.5403   C2003-910241-6
PR9199.3.Q34F76 2003

Library of Congress information is available upon request

Earlier versions of some of these pieces have appeared in *Equinox*,
Cottage Life, *Harrowsmith* and *Outdoor Canada*.

Editing by Barbara Pulling
Copy-editing by Michael Carroll
Jacket design by Paul Hodgson/pHd
Jacket photograph © Tyler Gourley/Getty Images/The Image Bank
Text design by Val Speidel
Printed and bound in Canada by Friesens
Printed on acid-free paper ∞
Distributed in the U.S. by Publishers Group West

We gratefully acknowledge the financial support of the Canada Council for the Arts, the
British Columbia Arts Council, and the Government of Canada through the Book
Publishing Industry Development Program (BPIDP) for our publishing activities.

For my beloved daughters, Carson and Flannery

Contents

Introduction

WHEN one is an angler, one receives many angling-related gifts. For example, I own many fish pens: many more than any man, even a guy who makes his living as a writer, would ever need. Likewise those plastic singing fishes. If you want one, just ask; they are all buried deep in boxes in my basement, and occasionally I'll toss aside a hammer or something only to be startled by a version of "Take Me to the River," made eerie by battery depletion, although I don't believe these automatons are ever going to die. And T-shirts, oh, my, I have quite a collection. Some are rather odd. I have one that reads THE TROUT, THE WHOLE TROUT, NOTHING BUT THE TROUT, SO HELP ME COD; people will often read my shirt front, their faces set in expectation of laughter, and then they will reread and their faces will fall and finally they will simply walk away. My favourite T-shirt has a Gary Larsen cartoon reprinted on it. Two fishermen sit in a little dinghy; much of the background is taken up by a dark nuclear mushroom cloud. One fisher is saying to the other, "I'll tell you what this means— no more size restrictions and to hell with the limit!"

And, of course, I have the T-shirt that boldly announces FISHING IS LIFE—EVERYTHING ELSE IS WAITING. One can purchase garments that make this proclamation about virtually every pastime and/or discipline: GOLF IS LIFE—EVERYTHING ELSE IS WAITING. SCUBA DIVING IS LIFE, GO-MOKU IS LIFE, NUDE CLOG DANCING IS LIFE—EVERYTHING ELSE IS WAITING. It is a bold and impassioned assertion, but I don't wear the T-shirt, at least, I have relegated it to duty as jogging wear, placing it in the same drawer as the shirt that reads MY BROTHER WENT TO HAWAII AND . . . (You know the drawer I mean.) I don't wear the shirt because I am old enough to remember that the statement is a version of one made by the great Karl Wallenda, who said, famously, "Life is being on the wire; everything else is waiting." The high wire, he meant, and we know what was waiting: a parked car in San Juan, Puerto Rico, which Karl bounced off after strong winds toppled him from a wire strung between two office buildings. I think what Karl should have said, what all these T-shirts should assert, is that everything else is waiting *to happen.*

Which is to say, I don't, I can't, endorse the bifurcation of angling and existence. The two are intimately bound for me, although there are different sorts of interweavings. When everything in my life is fine and good, fishing becomes a celebration, my senses harmonizing with the surroundings. When life becomes turbulent, fishing is a respite, troubles driven away by single-mindedness. (Everything is life, fishing is waiting.) And when things are downright miserable, the repetitive nature of the pursuit can approximate ceremony, ritual, and small, sad gods come to stand along the riverside.

So while all these pieces are about fishing, they're not *all about fishing*, if you see what I mean. For one thing, I don't fish particularly well, so instead of writing about why I'm catching any particular fish (which I rarely am), I often speculate on why I fish at all. And this is bound inextricably with my life and its vagaries. If I am sometimes in the Bahamas with my friend Jake, it is because I have fled a huge stinking mess at home. In other instances, I may have been pounded by professional setbacks or garden-variety bad luck. So it is that you will learn, in the pieces themselves and in little italicized asides, some personal details; you will suffer through my ruminations upon them.

I'm hoping that this elevates my work from the instructional to the devotional.

Not that what will follow is all gloom and despair; I will not linger on the parked cars that line the netless beneath. There will be moments of great joy. Some of these pieces were commissioned originally, and let me tell you, it is a great joy to go off fishing and have someone else pay for it. It is a great joy to go through customs and have the following discourse with the crew-cutted official.

"And what do you do for a living, Mr., um, *Quare*ington?"

"I'm a writer."

"What sort of writer?"

"An *outdoors* writer."

At which point the official invariably smiles and hands back my letters of transit. Nice work if you can get it, indeed.

I remember vividly my first such assignment. The editor of the fine magazine *Equinox* phoned up and said, "Hello, Paul? Listen, we're interested in the West Coast sportfishing scene, and what we were thinking was to send a writer out there to one of the grand old lodges to fish for a week or so. What do you think of that idea? Paul? Paul, are you there? Does this interest you at all? Paul?"

"Oh, I'm going to say *yes*," I replied, "just as soon as I'm done giggling."

STEELHEAD DREAMS

I AM perched in the bow of a drift-boat, a dory shaped like a silly grin, bouncing over rocks and white water. My fingers are tightened around the gunwales. The guide, John Elzinga—significantly, a former rodeo rider—sits serenely between the oars, every so often pulling the blades through the riffle, a process that over time and distance moves the vessel from one side of the Cowichan River to the other. Yesterday, our first day on the river, I asked John what motivated this piloting, and I received an answer I didn't much care for. Two young men—boys, really, eighteen or nineteen years of age—had ventured down the wrong side of the river. They were driven toward a sinister elbow and into a huge clay bank. The boat overturned and one of the boys was lost. "The Cowichan can be," John told me, "pretty unforgiving."

It is the end of March, and the water is fast and high. The Cowichan (one of the most famous, and fishy, waterways on British Columbia's Vancouver Island) is not in particularly good *shape*, that being a term employed by steelheaders to describe many things about a river, chiefly its colour, but also its size and force, maybe even its mood on any given day. Rain has fallen in the days previous, rendering the Cowichan brownish and determined. Ever since a flood last year, the banks fall away easily and the river is quick to blow out, but some sunny weather this morning has the water settling down and regaining its emerald cast.

Steelheaders not only have their own lexicon (*blow out* above is an example; a river in particularly poor shape might be *spewing chunks*), they are an altogether fascinating subspecies of Izaak Walton's Piscator. They sport neoprene chest waders, layers of sweaters and jackets (steelheading is largely a winter sport on the West Coast) and baseball caps. Steelheaders are forever emerging from rivers wearing expressions of dazed ecstasy, as if what they just experienced was part baptism, part roller-coaster ride. I come from Ontario, where angling has a staid civility. Pickerel are sober-sided fish: they pick at the bait in an overly fussy manner, and when hooked they often come to the boat with fatalistic ease. I have seen no looks of loopy transcendence on the faces of my eastern fishing compatriots.

That's why I am trying to become a steelheader.

Yesterday John and I fished the upper section of the river above Skutz Falls, four-wheel-driving to it on old logging roads and a long strip of gravel that once bedded railway ties. I had optimistically taken my fly-fishing gear, because the water in Block 51 (the Forestry designation) was reported to be much clearer and somewhat slower. "Somewhat slower" was still much faster than I could handle. My yarn fly was pulled rather harmlessly beneath the surface and only neared the bottom at the bank, there to become imbedded in the roots and branches of tumbled trees. I shortened my leader and tied in a weighted section. I tried to throw an S-cast, a technique that would lay down my line in a series of serpentine curves; the time required to straighten the line would also allow it to sink. Unfortunately this required a skill I had either lost or never acquired, so in desperation I affixed a small piece of shot near the fly. When I began casting, all this extra load imparted a violent, herky-jerky motion to the line, as though the fly were steroid-addled. John pointed helpfully toward where he thought fish might be; in this case, in the river rather than the moss-covered cottonwoods.

Soon John spotted—I stood by his side and squinted—a russet shape sitting near the bottom. I eagerly fired a succession of offerings, most of which were swept over the fish's head. Those that made it near him were disdained. He was by no means inactive, our fish; when another shape drifted near, he pushed out like a left tackle, forcing the intruder off to one side. He then resumed his post. From beside him came a quick flash of silver, and we understood that he was not alone. Another fish, chromed so as to mirror the environment and disguise her in the river, was digging out a redd.

I laid aside my fishing gear.

STEELHEAD are, technically speaking, anadromous rainbow trout, *anadromous* denoting their singular travel up and down the river. In the common British Columbia parlance, they are listed with the salmons, for they share some of the life experience. After a year or two in a parent river, the steelhead fry become smolts—a process that allows their systems to deal with salt water—and they put out to sea. Three years later they are directed back by those enigmatic inner urges, back to their home river and spawning grounds, there to perform what would seem to be one of the least satisfying acts of procreation in the animal kingdom. As the male hangs dutifully nearby to drive away interlopers, the female digs out the redd and deposits her eggs. Next the male drifts over and fertilizes the eggs with milt. And that's that, at least for the salmon who, wasted by the journey, their bodies consumed as sustenance for their own life juices, simply die.

The steelhead, however, heals and regains strength. A fish that has spawned and recuperated is called a *mended kelt.* It puts out to sea once more and returns to spawn again. Some even go and come home a third time. And as great a marvel as this is, there is a crude corollary: steelhead become *large.*

The magical division line is somewhere around fifteen pounds. Below that weight the fish are sprightly and fun to battle. Above fifteen pounds they become power sources, and their strength grows exponentially with size, so as they near the upper parameter (thirty-five pounds, say) they become virtually impossible to land on angling tackle. My guide, John, estimates that perhaps 70 per cent of fish over fifteen pounds are not brought to possession. Accordingly, losing a fish is not freighted with the same rueful shame that it is back east. The fish are going to be released back to the river, anyway. You're permitted to keep a small number of hatchery fish (ten per year), but all of the wild steelhead must be put back, and the barbs have been removed from the hooks to aid in this. (The adipose fin has been clipped on a hatchery fish; that's how you tell the difference.) The size and power of steelhead account in some measure for the giddy expressions their pursuers wear. They are among the elite of sport fishes, as prized a catch as the world has to offer, up there with muskies and tarpon. Had I managed to take one on the fly, it would qualify to some as a major life achievement. But I did not, and am not likely to in the fast water of the lower river, where my own equipment is useless.

So I have adjusted (kind of) to more standard steelheading gear. Tackle evolves much like the fish it is meant to take; it acquires charms and requires skills all its own. My rod is ten and a half feet long, two and a half feet of that being corked butt. In the saddle sits a bait-casting reel, the kind worked so adeptly by bass fishermen, the kind that we Ontario walleye boys look upon with humble dread. The reel requires a certain soft thumbing, or else the spool overrevolves and spits forth a dense knot of monofilament. The situation is exacerbated by the fact that there is anywhere from eight to fourteen feet of free line left dangling at the other end. The line is stopped at the rod tip by a bobber of some kind (mine is a Styrofoam tube, gaudily chartreuse) and then some weights (two or three split-shot, an egg sinker; I have a short section of pliable lead). A swivel connects a two-foot lead of lighter line, ten-pound test to the main twelve. The terminal tackle is what lends the outfit its allure and elevates the sport, because it consists only of the small barbless hook and an eloquent representation of roe. Mine is a wooden bead, essentially a pink-orange "corky."

The corky is flipped into the river, and this act is for me very like fly-fishing, for there is ample opportunity to leave most of your tackle in a nearby tree. Much of the fishing is done from the shore and shallows, standing backed up to the cottonwoods. Hence, you must imagine a hypothetical trajectory that sails the line through the branches safely. You develop a repertoire of deliveries: sidearm, underhanded, Gadabout Gaddis's bow-and-arrow technique. I have even managed to become admirably ambidextrous, switching to my left hand if the background to that side is sparser. There is another factor at play, I'll admit, in that my right arm is often about to fall off. Steelhead require a vast multitude of casts.

My first casts are made to wherever John suggests. He knows each section of river intimately, knows its structure, history and eccentricities. Steelhead commonly occupy the tail-out of a run, but at a particular hole something might draw them farther up, so John indicates areas of concentration. The cast is made gently upstream. The reel is left on free-spool so that the bait bounces down over rock and root and past the mouth of a steelhead, who is opportunistically sitting there, waiting for the current to deliver his dinner. At least that's the theory, but should John's instruction prove unproductive, you next look at the surface for a seam in the water, a place where two flows meet. The steelhead like to park just inside the slower water. At least that's the theory. When *that* fails, you cover as much water as you can and try for steelhead who aren't aware of these theories. You keep tight contact, both physically and visually, with your bobber, and when it pops underwater, you pull back hard. This is to set the hook, although it also serves to set your tackle into dead branches and between rocks.

JOHN Elzinga begins pulling the oars and the drift-boat moves off to one side of the Cowichan, drawing a slow hypotenuse from the middle of the river to the bank. Roiling gravel bounces from the bottom of the dory, producing a sound like radio static. The mountains around us are hidden by what is either heavy mist or low, brooding cloud. The trees are second-growth, but they already seem ancient: tall, gnarly and grizzled with lichen. I ask John to name the indigenous trees for me—alder, fir, hemlock. Alerted by an alien beeping, I ask him to tell me if he hears any noteworthy wildlife. "Okay," he agrees, cocking his head toward the wood. "That's a robin."

Each stopping place on the river has also been named. Wash

Out, Durance's, Biting Dog, Bible Camp, Cahoots, Cedar Log, Non-Productive, Leaning Fir. I might add "Etc." if there were any kind of overriding logic at work. Some names are obvious enough; Wash Out is a crooked dogleg where the river has razed the surrounding flora. Wash Out changed during last year's flood, so there are now two holes instead of one—Upper and Lower Wash Out. An optimistic soul is building a house there; the skeletal frame clings somewhat desperately to the road beyond. The banks are fortified with riprap, a bridge mixture of large rocks and small boulders intended to deflect the river. It is also the name some of the younger fishermen have given to Durance's, ignorant of the fact that the Durance family abided there for years. (Although it is not necessary to live at a spot to earn the eponym; Hankins Hole has been called that for thirty years because, as John explains, "The Hankins were always fishing it.") Riprap is what one lady on the river refuses to have dumped on the banks. The Cowichan is tired of swinging around her property and is fairly insistent about banging out a new, more direct course, but her attitude is that she has no business interfering with nature and God's will. One day soon the river will break through and, in a rare case of poetic injustice, head straight for the home of the man who runs the Bible Camp.

The names can confuse things. On our first trip down the river John had rounded a corner and exclaimed, "Where's the cedar log? There used to be a huge cedar log here." It had apparently been taken elsewhere by the river. John wondered about its disappearance for a good while, expecting to meet it around each bend. Then we put into shore, and as I fished, I asked, "What's this place called?"

"Cedar Log."

I took a long and careful look around. "Where's the cedar log?"

"There hasn't been a cedar log at Cedar Log for years."

I know some of the spots by idiosyncratic names. Ranch Del Rio (there was once a dude ranch there) I call "Dirty Buck" because I grappled with a fish there, a large male wearing a gaudy coat of mottled spawning colours. He leapt out of the water, infuriated, and the hook popped free of its kype. As I sat there tsking my tongue the fish made a second leap, pirouetting and splashing down hard, and it was difficult not to believe he was communicating great umbrage. "Big dirty buck," John commented.

Bucks and *does* are what we call them, the bucks splashed with colour, the does silver as tinfoil. I was not used to differentiating fish in this manner, and (although I will be accused of anthropomorphism, and probably justly) there is a sense in which steelhead seem more complex, evolved, even intelligent. Once at Lower Wash Out I hooked a big fish, and as I braced for the engagement I noticed with dismay that my line was wrapped around the rod tip. This seemed to mean certain loss of the fish and probable destruction of equipment, but for some reason the fish rested patiently and allowed me to work it all out. I turned the rod over in my hands until the line fell free. Then the fish seemed to say, "All right? All right," and headed downstream. I thumbed the spool in order to dissuade him (it turned out to be a buck of nine or ten pounds), blistering my thumb in the process.

WE pull over to the Runs below Robson. John reaches behind, tugging the pulley rope free, and a huge piece of lead, an inverted pyramid, falls into the water. I take a peek into the river, can see nothing but motion. "Should I get out of the boat?"

"I wouldn't," advises my guide. "It's about twelve feet deep."

I cast from the drift-boat into the river, allowing my little corky to bounce down toward the sea.

The weather has been confused today, clouding over, raining halfheartedly, clearing briefly and then doing it all over again, but the sun now makes an emphatic entrance, refreshed and eager to be about its business. The world seems to stretch and yawn at moments like this. Certainly John and I stretch and yawn, and as we are doing this we see a fairly wondrous thing. Two big fish leap out of the water with all the synchronicity of well-practised, nose-plugged swimmers. It is rare enough to see a steelhead leap—as John figures it, they have no real reason to—but two at the same time is at least fairly wondrous.

I make a second cast at the Runs below Robson with renewed optimism. I actually make it with the kind of hunch that lives next door to dead certainty. My corky's passage down the river is, however, uninterrupted. As I think about retrieving it, the bobber disappears suddenly. I jerk back, and it seems that at the same instant the fish humps out of the river, a fresh doe in excess of the magical fifteen pounds. It is in this instant that I begin to understand the sport.

The fish comes out of the water, driving toward the sun. It is hard to imagine how she prepared underwater for this manoeuvre; so perpendicular is the shaft of muscle, I suspect giddily that she was fired out of the water, launched off some elastic stretched between two rocks. Contact has yet to be made; I cannot connect this fish, some 150 feet away, with the rod in my hand. The fish settles back into the Cowichan, down into the current, and we are engaged.

When people ask me why I fish, it is this moment that I try to describe, an instant when I am tied to a life form, a life force. Hunters never know this, which is why I do not endorse the all-too-frequent pairing, NO HUNTING AND FISHING. If literature is meant to engage our emotions, exercising more rarified sensibilities like mercy and grief, then fishing is the activity for the fundamental feelings. It is plunging your finger into the beating heart of something. I suppose some would say that I am waxing over-poetical in describing the panicked twitches of a hooked fish, but to me it is a positive energy, a pure and glorious determination. And certainly this steelhead, now some 200 feet away and travelling, is determined. She is trying to light out for the territories, to ride the roaring current to freedom. I am trying to forestall her. My right thumb is clamped down on the spool, my other thumb is clamped down over it, but line is still being pulled away. With a certain lack of confidence, I pull up hard, plant the butt in my belly, use one of my hands to support the rod higher on the shaft. A strenuous balance is thereby achieved, and the fish is more or less stilled. There is the occasional creaking away of line, but otherwise the fish and I exist in a state of, well, I believe the scientific term is *stasis*. I put this to John in simpler terms. "I don't think there's much I can do here. She's strong."

John nods. He considers drawing up the anchor, but once he's done that we will be consigned to all the water below us, and this run will be lost. There's no going back on the Cowichan. You can put in again, later or the following day, but the river will be changed. And John and I don't want to leave this hole, because it is here that we saw that fairly wondrous thing, the two fish breaching in unison. So John does not draw up the anchor. The Cowichan River pushes past, full of ageless resolve. I hold on to my fishing rod and try to fabricate plans and courses of action. The steelhead has her plan all set out and sees no reason to alter it, except to swing across the river bottom into the passing lane, an unseen sluice of even quicker water. The line breaks and she is gone.

It has been said of mountains that they yield their secrets reluctantly. Sometimes a river does not yield its secrets at all. You are left properly humbled and distanced from its treasures. But when you come away from the river, there may be a strange new expression on your face, in equal parts foolishness and enlightenment.

THIS ONE

THIS one is about sneaking
    alongside a white brick bungalow
past windows propped open,
the gauzy curtain sucked into the moist dawn,
past the couple sleeping
there like two felled trees softened by moss
through the back yard
where a beer can lies tumbled, drunk,
over the green twist-tie fence
down the slope, shopping-carted, condomed,
across a path made by wheels,
man's fiercest invention,
through thuggish weeds
finally stumbling upon
a creek
four feet wide.

That's what this one is about.

POACHING WITH MY OLD GUY

M Y parents own a beautiful piece of land in eastern Ontario. About two miles to the south of it lies Lake Ontario, and the lake and the land are connected by a stream. The stream is rather ambitious near the big water, pushing through farmers' fields with a certain amount of stateliness, but by the time it arrives at my parents' place it could more properly be called a *rill*. I am not even sure what a rill is, exactly, but it suits this: a small creek so meandering as to seem lost and confused. Still, the rill holds a few trout, and I am a fisherman (I speak not of skill but of devotion to the Art of the Angle) because of that rill.

Occasionally I have run off poachers. I am alerted by strange sounds coming from the hills—poachers sneaking down to plunder the rill. I come upon them with stern words and foul language. I screw up my face to suggest advanced lunacy. Most simply turn back when asked to leave, sometimes blinking and looking around as if they had been somnambulating and are as surprised as anyone to find themselves standing in an alien wood. A few argue, claiming there were no signs (which is usually true, as they have torn them down) or expanding on some arcane bit of law.

A fellow once informed me that since one could not own waterways, he was therefore entitled to any fish he could pull out of them. I countered that the statute did not apply to rills, which did not satisfy him. All of this leads to my big solution to the problem. I borrow my sister-in-law's dog Jessie from time to time. Jessie is enormous and does not like interlopers. She will cock her head briefly, rush off with a series of stentorian heralds, and the surrounding hills will suddenly come alive with furious scurrying.

I SHALL now tell you how all this pertains to Gordon, my Old Guy. (Those of you unfamiliar with the term *Old Guy* might want to refer to an earlier book of mine, *Fishing with My Old Guy*. Mind you, the meaning is likely not all that mysterious: a mentor, a guru, a magus, although in this somewhat unmagical age, it's best to just say Old Guy.)

Gordon is not that old, by the way, sixty-something, but I hope you see that age has little to do with it. Gordon is a world-class fly caster, a maker of rods, a tier of flies, a lover of nature. And when I say *lover of nature*, I mean to raise the ante on that particular term. I never met a man who was so attuned to the natural world. In a way, he does not exist on the same planet as the rest of us. Gordon has an ability to disregard buildings amid hydro towers, to simply not see them, with Mr. Magoo's blessed innocence, registering instead the proverbial *lay of the land*. At the same time he will spot little things that might escape the notice of a team of binoculared scientists.

Here is the sort of thing Gordon does. Say we were driving along somewhere north of Toronto, having spent the morning fishing a small creek, um, somewhere north of Toronto. (I am not being secretive here. Gordon's favoured time of departure for fishing trips is several minutes after I have managed to get to sleep. I am usually too groggy to remember much beyond general direction.) Gordon drives a huge American motoring sedan, a great-finned land shark, which he pilots as if it were a jeep or a four-by-four, blithely driving off the road and into the wilderness, staring straight ahead.

He will point out things as we pass by. There are big things, things that even I notice. Fields, for example. Gordon adores huge, empty, flat fields, which has to do with his casting practice. Tournament casting has six distance events, and when you start wielding a thirty-foot salmon rod over your head, you need a little elbow room.

Gordon also likes streams. "There's a good one!" he will exclaim. Often they appear to me to be nothing more than rills, but Gordon will go on at some length. In the time it takes him to drive by, and without turning his head, Gordon will note any number of features: felled trees, undercuts, small burns, all places that hold fish.

Gordon remarks on every stream and field that we pass by,

which, if you happen to be driving all the way to Cincinnati with him, can become a little annoying. I did happen to be driving all the way to Cincinnati with him (for a casting tournament) and at one point remarked acidly on his predilection. "I like fields, and I like streams," he acknowledged. "And, God, I love that magazine."

But I have committed a huge writerly faux pas, leaping from a car somewhere north of Toronto to a car heading down to Cincinnati. It was the same car, but that is no excuse. So there are these large observations Gordon makes. Then there is this sort: "Did you see that fox?"

Fox? Sometimes it takes me a moment to locate whatever *field* Gordon is referring to. During my car trips with Gordon, we have driven by every creature, great and small, that abides in this fair land. I have seen none of them; Gordon has noticed all of them, without turning his head. Gordon claims to possess exceptional peripheral vision, and it is true that he is a hard guy to sneak up on. (I often try to disprove his claim.)

You are probably asking yourselves, how do you know he is not lying? I do not, really, except that from time to time Gordon will notice something that makes him slam on the brakes, stopping his huge motor sedan somewhere near the soft shoulder. This could be one of two things. It could be a road kill, which Gordon will gleefully scrape up and toss into the trunk of his motoring sedan. What he wants, you understand, is the fur or feathers (which the owner no longer needs) to use as fly-tying materials.

The other thing that will cause Gordon to stop is the sighting of food. (There have been a few ghastly occasions when the line between the two got a little blurry, but I will not go into it now.) Gordon believes that much of the world is edible. To be fair, what Gordon believes is that there are things to eat out there, delicious and free, which most people drive by without noticing. (He has written quite a good book on the subject, although he does suggest a few things that I think might have had even Euell Gibbons, noted forager, he of *Stalking the Wild Asparagus,* scurrying for the flounder box.)

Let me illustrate by returning to somewhere north of Toronto. I am sitting (groggily), not noticing anything; Gordon has remarked on hawks, hairy toads, lemurs and leopards (or something like that). Suddenly he throws on the brakes and pulls the car into geographical proximity of the soft shoulder.

"Look!" he says, pointing at a field. "Puffballs!"

I manage to spot the field—the white fence is a giveaway—and am willing to accept that there are puffballs in it. I am not willing to leap the fence and claim them, particularly when two large mastiffs run up and defend their side of the fence with bared teeth and maniacal ululations. Gordon starts climbing.

"Don't worry about them," he says. "Look at their tails."

Their tails make a vague wagging motion, almost imperceptible, likely the result of a small breeze. But when Gordon drops into their midst, the dogs look at each other in bewilderment. The barking and fang-baring have always done the trick before. Having exhausted their repertoire, the hounds turn away dejectedly and Gordon pulls puffballs.

So you see, in my Old Guy, certain characteristics, including a unique relationship with nature and (I am sure this did not go unnoticed) something of a disregard for the concept of private property.

Now it came to pass one summer's day that Gordon and I went fishing. "I'll see you here at five o'clock," he said, meaning his house, meaning in the morning. Gordon himself goes to bed around eight. He does not understand night owls like me who might like to stay up and see what Peter Mansbridge has to report. I managed to make it to his house by five, although I arrived heavy-lidded, confused and unable to form complete sentences. The good thing about Gordon's earth boat is that it is spacious and comfy, so as soon as we pulled out of the drive, I drifted off.

I awoke what I suppose was about two hours later, and I awoke for this reason: Gordon had blithely turned the car off the road. He did not run off the freeway onto a two-lane, or off a two-lane onto a dirt road; no, he turned off a dirt road onto unadulterated topography. When he does this sort of thing, he affects the air of a person out for a Sunday drive, drumming his fingers on the steering wheel, whistling tunelessly.

He stopped at the edge of a gorge, and we climbed out of the car and looked at the river. I suppose I could name it, but for some reason I am reluctant to. It is a good river, well known. Where it is crossed by the Macdonald-Cartier Freeway (which the highway accomplishes via a bridge of great length), the river is wide and violent, all white water and concrete abutments. Farther north it turns quiet. Where Gordon and I stood, the river was perhaps twenty feet across. We stood at an elbow, where time had made the water shallow and formed a sandbar. Standing on the sandbar and looking farther north still, we saw that the river made itself even smaller and wandered into the shadowy woods.

We followed it there, but not before putting on our stuff. One of the auxiliary pleasures of the Art of the Angle is the putting on of stuff. My own stuff was fairly new: I had scientifically advanced neoprene hip waders, Polaroid sunglasses and a fishing vest that was, for all intents and purposes, one of those stylish multipocketed photojournalist jackets, except for a little patch of fuzz to stick flies on and a few extra pockets.

Gordon's own hip waders were rendered out of whatever was used before they discovered rubber. His fishing vest was weathered (I have just been to the thesaurus and am disappointed to find that there are not words like *typhooned* or *hurricaned* to employ in this case). It was zipperless and may or may not have retained some buttons. It was impossible to tell, because Gordon wore the contents of a Canadian Tire franchise on it. From the shoulders streamed long pieces of twine with split-shot crimped on, which somehow lent Gordon a quasi-military aspect. Dangling from the vest were some tools: knives, nail clippers, hook removers, pliers, a thick piece of rubber for straightening leaders. Oh, that's right, he wore leaders on his vest, tiny loops of line ordered in some manner; the vest was also bedecked with a multitude of tiny flies, and, in case he hadn't brought the precise one he needed, some of his vest pockets were filled with fur and feathers so that Gordon could whip up the required fly streamside. Other pockets were crammed with hooks, lures, floats, swivels, weights, line and spare reel parts.

And Gordon wore a hat, an old Andy Capp thing, that made him look as if he had a road kill balanced on top of his head.

The sky was empty, the sun had been awakened early, the day was already toasty. If we had been observed by alien eyes—I often have this thought, *What would a Venusian think?*—I am sure we would have added to humankind's already eccentric reputation. "There it was, thirty-five degrees Celsius, and these guys were dressed up in *rubber*."

I will tell you how Gordon fishes a river: on tiptoe. He inches his way along and spends very little time actually putting line to water. Gordon will simply judge a piece of river and quickly decide where the fish are likely to be. Now, as a rule of thumb, I can report that fish are likeliest to be where it is difficult, if not impossible, to place a fly or lure. This is where it comes in pretty handy being the North American Masters Casting Champion, which Gordon had been for many years previous.

Gordon also benefits from some practice at a pastime called

Arrenburg, which is a European casting game designed to test streamside skills. Casts are made underhanded, from the side, just as they must be when the angler is confined and constricted by brush. So while Gordon tiptoed and cast with breathtaking precision, I plodded along behind, still half-asleep, distributing terminal tackle in various branches, a fact I mention because I suppose at some point during the initial stages of the fishing, Gordon and I went over, under or through some manner of barricade, boundary or fence.

We came to a little crook in the river, edging toward it as if the river itself were a skittish deer and likely to bolt at any time. Gordon saw something that cracked his face apart with a smile. He pulled me back, well out of the water's earshot, and gesticulated wildly.

"The tree, the tree," he whispered.

A tree had fallen, keeled over headfirst like a drunk at dawn, and lay half in and half out of the water. These were trout digs if ever there were trout digs, and Gordon was offering me first crack at them. Gordon always offered me first crack. I usually offered it right back, especially if the preamble went anything like, "Can you see the undercut just behind that gnarly mass of briar, all of which is obscured from view by this enormous weeping willow? Cast there."

However, I had a chance at this felled tree. And, I should mention, precisely that—a single chance. I was casting a tiny Mepps lure, and my first and only cast would either (a) convince the fish that a large and juicy bug had tumbled from a branch,[*] or (b) announce the arrival of yet another clumsy angler. ([*]Here is one of Gordon's tips, offered just in case you hoped you might learn something about fishing by reading this story: remove that little bit of red tubing that Mepps puts on the shank of the hook, because it destroys the tumblebug illusion.) At any rate, I remembered as well as I could Gordon's various instructions—he was, after all, my Old Guy—and managed a neat little flick that plopped musically near the felled tree. I saw the fish drift out to investigate.

They say Ted Williams could see the seams on a baseball as it came at him in the batter's box, and I seem to have acquired something of this preternatural visual ability, seeing things with astounding clarity and in slow motion, for I saw the fish look at the lure and decide, "Oh-oh, stupid fishermen . . ." I gave the line a little twitch then, and the lure jerked in the fish's face. The fish said, "Hold on here," and ate that tumbling bug in a flash.

Then it hightailed it.

One often sees fishermen following their fish downstream or upstream, quivering rods held out in front like dowsing sticks. These nimrods tramp through the water, screaming, "Fish on!" to other anglers (which is to say, "Clear out of the way!"), acting as if their trout were part St. Bernard and in need of its daily perambulation. Gordon views this with a fair measure of disdain, his thinking being that if one is willing to follow the fish long enough, one is likely to claim it. Gordon is nothing if not sporting, and for that reason, he stands his ground, refusing to budge, and if he is your Old Guy, that is the sort of thing that is expected.

The fish on the other end of my line was not a behemoth, please do not misunderstand, but it was a three-pound rainbow trout, and its fury bent my rod over sharply. My first thought was that if I could walk it down to Lake Ontario, it might give up out of boredom. Gordon touched my arm, staying me on the bank, and fastened his eyes to the water. Like many fine anglers, Gordon has the ability to see into water, to correct optically for the refraction and reflection, and he gave me the somewhat alarming news that the fish was headed for a submerged tree stump as gnarly with roots as Medusa's head. Gordon was giggling as he gave me this news, delighted with my good fortune.

"Lower your rod," he advised urgently—it is hard to sound urgent and giggle at the same time, but Gordon managed it—and then he gently guided my rod down until it lay parallel to the horizon, still wowed and aquiver, and in this manner was the fish dissuaded from the stump, its escape coming to naught. In some minutes, the fish joined Gordon and me—by now we were both giggling—on the shore. We stopped giggling in order to dispatch the fish, which we did with both celerity and solemnity.

It was then that the hound from hell made its appearance. It seems to me that the cur must have been hanging in the trees while all this was going on. The animal dropped into our midst with raised hackles, bared teeth and flashing eyes. Its tail was not wagging, not even the slightest bit. It did not bark, other than a single eloquent yawp that razored through my innards. I am not sure of Gordon's reaction—I was too busy watching my life flash before my eyes—but I suspect that he remained placid, seeing at once the poetry of his existence being snuffed out by a slobbering mastiff.

We were spared by its master's voice—"Bob!"—but I figured we were still in deep trouble, not trusting anyone who would name his dog *Bob*. And when the man appeared—was he too hanging from the trees, just waiting to pounce?—my suspicions were confirmed. He was enormous, for one thing, with unruly hair and dark grey eyes. He advanced on us evenly, each footfall heavy and ominous. OBSCURE WRITER AND HIS OLD GUY, the headlines would read, perhaps not on the front page, MURDERED BY SERIAL KILLER.

"Hey!" barked the man. (I think it was him; it may have been the dog.) "What have you got behind your back?"

"Oh, nothing," said I.

"Good morning, sir, and a wonderful morning it is!" Gordon piped up.

"What is it?" the man demanded of me once more. "Is it a fish?"

"Oh, say, yes, it is a fish!"

"Poachers," the man snarled. I believe he may have added an adjective or two.

"Are we on your land?" asked Gordon with a large dollop of stagy innocence.

"It's my land," said he, "and my fish." He held out his hand, and I meekly tendered the catch, which nestled with frightening ease in the palm.

Gordon removed his road-kill cap and scratched at his head. "We must have got lost in the woods," he suggested.

"I don't believe you got lost in the woods," said the man, "but you're going to get lost now. *Bob . . .*"

So get lost we did, at a world-record pace, and soon the two of us were hiking along a country road, fishing rods slung over our shoulders. The red-winged blackbirds perched on their bulrushes seemed to taunt us as we walked by. Gordon was grinning. I was red-faced and fuming.

"I can't believe it," I muttered. "I can't believe I'm a *poacher.*"

"Poaching," said my old guy, "has a long and honourable history."

I stopped and wondered what Gordon meant by that. And suddenly I understood. I do not think I would have understood on a day that was not so gorgeous. There was a stillness, except for Gordon and me tramping down a road, roasting under the sun in our rubberwear. The world was wide awake but curiously lazy. It had hung a sign where its business shingle should have been: GONE FISHING. Gordon and I have been forced off one tiny piece of the planet, but it was a beautiful planet and very, very large. I understood then why Gordon grinned all the time, because I found myself grinning. This story is about learning that from my Old Guy.

So I understood his statement totally, utterly, but only for that wonderful while. I have not turned into an anarchic angler. I abide by the law. But these days when I hear the sounds coming from the woods at my parents' place—they are giggles mostly—I usually go indoors and read a book for an hour or two. When I come back out, all is silent once more.

THE ENFORCER

WRAY McQuay is a conservation officer, but he doesn't mind referring to himself as a game warden. Older people relate to that term better, he's found, or people using English as a second language. Just as long as they understand who he is, McQuay reasons, and what he does. What he does on this particular June day is put his boat, a sixteen-footer with a seventy-horsepower Evinrude, into the heavily fished waters of Lake Scugog. It is a fine Sunday, warm and comfortable, unlike the week preceding it, which had the broiling fierceness of high summer. (It is not high summer significantly—bass season has not opened.)

McQuay is one of five conservation officers working out of the Lindsay office of the Ontario Ministry of Natural Resources (MNR). He has been with the ministry for twenty-four years, and "in the field," as he puts it, for an even twenty, although some of his time—too much time, he thinks—is spent in the office, attending to paperwork. One or two days a month he's in the courthouse, offering up evidence against poachers he's caught. (I use the term as McQuay does, to describe someone who transgresses government hunting and fishing rules. I do not use it in its more restricted but commonly accepted sense, i.e., a person who sneaks onto another's property to catch a small fish or two. We've all done that, haven't we?) McQuay is outdoors the remainder of the time, overseeing angling, hunting and the alteration of shoreline or fisheries habitat. Many people, although right-thinking, do a great deal of damage while building around their cottages, dumping sand over gravelly spawning grounds, for example, or clearing away the weeds and reeds that serve as fishy housing projects. And even a cottager blithely firing a little Mepps from his dock must be able to produce a fishing licence if asked to by a conservation officer. McQuay has alarmed a number of people by motoring right up to their docks and doing just that.

McQuay's bailiwick consists of six lakes: Sturgeon, Balsam, Mitchell, Cameron, Canal and this popular and well-used one near Port Perry, Ontario. His own cottage is on Head Lake—near, but not in, his district—where he enjoys fly-fishing for bass.

McQuay strikes out for the nearest anglers, five people in a small aluminum boat. He rises behind the steering console as he makes his approach, his eyes working quickly, registering the number of lines in the water, looking for a stringer or a suddenly liberated fish. McQuay has a military bearing, suggested by his well-cropped but bristly moustache and heavily underscored by the Smith & Wesson he wears at his hip. The anglers are clearly nervous; they stare at their lines with abject disinterest, as though fishing were the last thing in the world they wanted to be doing that morning. McQuay does his best to put them at ease, hailing them affably and speaking as quietly as possible: "I'm just going to pull up alongside you there and check your licences." When the boats are side by side, McQuay places one foot on their gunwale and repeats his request.

Two adult males in the boat—there are also two younger males, and a young female—rummage through tackle boxes. One produces a neatly folded yellow piece of paper, which McQuay opens and scans quickly, nodding then with satisfaction. The other man comes up with an Outdoors Card, a hard plastic affair that looks like a Visa or an American Express, except that it has a wonderfully sylvan scene emblazoned across it. The yellow piece of paper is what you receive when you first purchase a licence; another copy is forwarded to the MNR, which then sends out your card. The second man looks momentarily pleased with himself, but his expression changes abruptly when McQuay flips the card over and says, "Oh-oh."

"You didn't get it renewed this season," McQuay continues. He indicates a series of boxes on the back, empty save for one. "You get a new sticker every year. It's like the plate for your car."

McQuay asks the man for his driver's licence. He sits down again and takes out his ticket book. As the angler offers excuses for his failure to renew, McQuay calmly makes out a ticket. When finished, he addresses the errant angler solemnly, telling him which courtroom to be in, and when, should he choose to contest the matter; telling him where to mail the fine, also. The other anglers in the boat, patently under the age of fourteen, are not required to have licences.

The writer crouched in the prow of the boat finds all this licence stuff very interesting, because he himself is ever neglectful. Many times he goes out fishing, and rarely does he have his Outdoors Card with him. Now he discovers that this transgression could cost him $80; indeed, due to the vagaries of the law, he would be better advised to claim never to have *had* a licence, the fine for which is a mere fifty clams.

Over the course of the morning, Wray McQuay proves himself not the martinet he might seem. As the conservation officer and the writer draw near one boat, the angler lays his rod down and lights a cigarette with grim fatalism.

"I'm going to pull up alongside you there and check your licence," McQuay calls over.

"Don't have it," the man confesses.

"Don't have it at all?"

"Don't have it on me. It's on my dresser. *Damn.*"

"Where did you buy it?"

"Huh? Oh, Canadian Tire."

"Which Canadian Tire?"

"In Whitby."

"How much did it cost?"

"I dunno. Twenty-five bucks, something like that."

This has the ring of authenticity. The temporary licence costs $15.50; the plastic Outdoors Card, an additional $6. They can be purchased in most tackle shops and marinas, although, judging from the anglers McQuay talked to that day, Canadian Tire has a crippling monopoly. The conservation officer nods and reaches for a small satchel. He rifles through and pulls out a business card.

"I try to go easy on one person every day," announces McQuay. "You're it. Now you fax me a copy of your licence before Wednesday and everything will be fine. If I don't receive it, I'll charge you with obstruction, providing a fisheries officer with false information. Not only that, but I'll come and arrest you personally." This is not an empty threat; a conservation officer's powers of seizure and arrest are awesome. Anything used in connection with the violation can be impounded. If the miscreant is catching out-of-season fish, for instance, a conservation officer can confiscate his or her boat and motor as evidence.

As Officer McQuay goes about his business, the writer, always a conscientious researcher, peppers him with questions. "Suppose you have one line in the water, you know, and nothing's biting, so you grab your casting rod and, you know, take a couple of casts, but you leave the other line in the water . . ."

McQuay grins craftily. "Is that what you do, Paul?"

"Oh, no! It's just hypothetical."

"A lot of times people lay one rod down on the bottom of the boat."

"Hey, that's pretty clever," I allow.

"But I notice the monofilament, sometimes even an extra bobber. That's how I get them."

"Right, right. Now, I was wondering about poaching. Not as in specific angling violations, but as in trespassing on someone else's land. That must be extremely hard to enforce, I bet. Anyway, it's not really that serious an offence, is it, Officer McQuay?"

He eyes me warily. "Hmmm," he hums.

Officer McQuay spends the afternoon inspecting livewells and stringers, looking for undersized muskies and any size of bass. Mostly he checks licences and issues tickets. He judges that the rate of offence on Lake Scugog is about 15 to 20 per cent. To the writer, however, the rate appears much higher. He has become sanctimonious by virtue of mere proximity to the conservation officer, scowling at offending anglers. He watches as a young man, bare-chested and sucking wheezily at a cigarette, reaches into his wallet and deftly extracts a valid Outdoors Card.

"Okay." McQuay nods toward the water behind the boat, where light colours flash a foot or so beneath the surface.

"You had a little luck there," he notes.

"Yeah."

"Why don't you pull that stringer up and let me take a look?"

The young man does so without reluctance. There is a pickerel, drowned by the fast water, and beside it, a largemouth bass.

"Oh-oh," says the writer, secretly pleased that the fellow has been caught afoul of the law.

"Do you know what kind of fish that is?" demands McQuay.

"I know, it's a bass. I wasn't going to take it out of the lake. I just wanted to show my friends over there." The young man nods vaguely across the water. "And then I was going to put it back."

"For one thing, I don't believe you. For another, that fish is dead."

The writer has a place on a river farther up north, and labour to do on that place. He'd been considering going up the next day and fishing during the evenings. Mostly for pickerel, of course, although he'd thought of taking a rather laissez-faire attitude concerning any bass that might chomp down on his lure.

He finds himself changing his mind, delaying the trip until the bass season is legally open. This is not so much because the young man's comeuppance is severe, although it certainly is. He is issued a summons to appear in court, his fishing rod is confiscated, and it is an act of mercy that McQuay doesn't impound the boat, rented from a nearby marina. More affecting for the writer is McQuay's grave censure.

"You know why I get so testy?" he asks the lad. "This is a big male that you caught. And now he's up here, dead, and not down there protecting the nest. And right now the rock bass are in there eating all the eggs and fry. So you didn't kill one bass. You killed a hundred bass."

As McQuay heads off, his face remains stony. Indeed, his face is sufficiently stony that the writer is reluctant to say anything, choosing instead to look at the fishing boats and savour the day. Finally, though, the silence must be broken. "You really care about this stuff, don't you?" the writer asks.

McQuay nods somberly, but then a large smile splashes across his face. "Hey," he points out, "if *I* don't care, who's going to?"

EQUIPPED TO THE GILLS

MANY folks, while not keen anglers, have the occasional yen or duty to go fishing. (You know what I mean by *duty*, don't you? Your Uncle Burl comes to visit the cottage, acting on an invitation uttered in a moment of semi-inebriated whimsy, and he is keen to test the waters.) This piece is my attempt to answer questions of equipage, to explain the mysteries of the tackle store. I am aware that this is a slightly seedy endeavour (along the lines of, *C'mon, kid, the first one's free*). Which is to say, I have a serious jones-on for angling gear and have invested several thousands of dollars in such stuff, dollars I have yet to actually earn. I promise here to stick with basic stuff, which is to say, tackle one might actually use.

To begin with, there is likely no need to start from scratch. Go to the big cupboard that I'm certain is there (I've never been to a cottage that didn't have one) and throw it open. Inspect the fishing gear as it comes tumbling out. At this point you're likely thinking: *What is this stuff, and who put it there?* Well, I don't know and I don't know. I suspect it was our forebears, but weren't they sensible and solemn folk? This gear, oversized and barbaric, appears to have been designed for arcane pursuits. Perhaps the lakes back then held monsters, coelacanths and sabre-toothed tiger fish; perhaps our forebears were simply more capable of dreaming large. Anyway, somewhere in that cupboard you're going to find something more suited to our modest ambitions, a rod of about five to six feet in length.

The reel is no doubt serviceable, once it's been cleaned with a cotton swab and the insides lubricated with a very lightweight oil, but the line is likely rotten, so tear it away, wrap it up tightly, tie it off and stuff it into your pocket for recycling. You must now go down to the tackle shop to get the reel refilled. While there, you're also going to buy what is called *terminal tackle,* the actual hooked gewgaws that entice the fish.

So march in with your empty reel and hand it to a friendly employee, asking if he or she would please fill it with eight-pound test monofilament. (You might not anticipate catching too many fish that weigh eight pounds, but the choice of line-test is predicated on the assumption that a fish, hoisted into the air and flipping about, exerts a force far greater than can be accounted for by body mass and gravity. Eight-pound test is also capable—if but barely— of handling any behemoths that may have eluded our forebears.) Not all stores offer this reel-filling service, mind you, but most clerks can be persuaded to do it, along with recycling your wadded-up snarl of old line for you. True, reel filling is a simple enough procedure, but I have my reasons for suggesting this course of action. First off, it might not be a complicated job, but it is a pain in the butt. More important, consider this: if the clerk nods happily, disappears into the back and returns in a couple of minutes with a freshly lined reel, you are obviously dealing with a pleasant, intelligent person whose help can be counted on. If the clerk either refuses or is stymied by the whole operation, he or she is not going to be of much use, anyway.

Fishing-tackle sections have a sameness, whether they occupy the whole of the sales floor or a shadowed corner in a huge hangar of hardware goods. The lures and packages of hooks are pegged up on holed half-walls. Beside and beneath them are strange devices, mystifying constructions of tin and lead. It is hard to accept at first that these strange things are appurtenances of angling. My advice: ignore everything but the wall. If they can't hang it up, you don't want it. Eschew the big stuff that needs to be stored in cribs. Your object is to catch as many fish as possible, and while a big fish may snap at a little bait, looking for a snack, a small fish very rarely attacks something large.

You are going to buy some lures, but only a scant few, things that fall within the two- to three-inch range. Buy a spoon, which is easy enough to spot, because it looks like a spoon, at least the business end of one. I might suggest the Williams Wabler, if only to see if that company will now give me a couple of free ones. Buy a crankbait, so-called because when using it you crank your reel, keeping the thing in constant motion. Most crankbaits are made to resemble a fish pretty realistically, although many lures don't appear to at first glance. Now, here is some useful advice that I must preface with a little anecdote. I once took my first daughter into a tackle shop when she was but a wee toddler. She stared at some ghastly amalgam of balsam and tin and said, "Fytz," by which she meant "fish." To me there was nothing even vaguely piscine about it. But I realized she was reacting to the shape, to the mere suggestion of fishiness. She was seeing as a fish does. This is what you must do. Don't be fooled by paint jobs that suggest verisimilitude. Take a step back and squint. See if anything jumps off the wall at you.

I'd also suggest two other considerations: sound and motion. Many of the crankbaits have little rattles inside them, which I think is a sound idea, and I swear to God I didn't mean to make that pun. Fish may lack external ears, but they're very sensitive to vibration, attracted to any "noise" that might come from a panicky little fingerling. Other lures are jointed, hinged so that they'll move through the water with the appropriate muscularity. You might also think about colouration; if the main forage food for the larger fish is the minnow, buy something silvery.

All right, then. You now have two or three lures. Next you must purchase some lead-headed jigs, if possible dressed with marabou or bucktail. They look like little balls of lead with a spray of fluff. At least that's what they look like to human beings who aren't employing the myopic method of shopping, stepping back and squinting to perceive the suggestion of fishiness. Imagine them suspended in the water, the fluff undulating nicely. Yummy. So buy a bunch. Check the packaging for the weight of the jig. You want them to weigh one-eighth or one-quarter of an ounce, handy all-purpose sizes. You could also buy some naked, unadorned jigs; experiment here with the colouring of the head. The basic head is silver, which is a good default choice, but many have been painted. I personally believe that fish are attracted to colours in the green-yellow-chartreuse band of the spectrum, but buy a few hot pinks too, because some days the fish are feeling undeniably flamboyant. Near the jigs you might also see little yellow pieces of rubber, most of which are designed to add more colour and movement to the overall presentation. Some of these have been saturated with scent, and most anglers agree this innovation is effective.

Plastic worms look pretty dumb, I guess, to the occasional angler, but bass seem to like them. I'm not saying that bass are fooled by them; I'm saying bass seem to enjoy the actual rubberiness of them, as if plastic were a rare delicacy for smallmouths. Perhaps the bass, feisty little contenders, sense in the bite of rubber some manner of resistance, which drives them wild. Plastic worms come in a dizzying array of colours; some are rainbowed by oil slicks, some are covered with glitter, but there's little point standing in the tackle shop trying to make a judicious selection. Different things work on different days; if blue isn't grabbing them, try the speckled puce.

Plastic worms have another great aspect to them, which I'll share with any parents who may be angling in the company of wee ones: children are fascinated with plastic worms. Never met a child who wasn't. So buy a lot and let the kiddies play with them as you fish.

As effective as plastic worms are, real ones do even better. In fact, live bait will succeed where all other methods fail, so it is best to prepare for that procedure. You need some hooks: long-shafted hooks, which are rated as #4s, or #6s, which generally represent a medium hook, big enough to carry a load, not so heavy as to anchor it to the bottom. (As a general rule, use #4s for minnows, #6s for worms.) Some people like to put a small bell sinker in front of the hook, which will help drag the bait down and make it snake in a more lifelike manner over the rocks and sunken logs. I suppose that's a good enough idea, but I don't really recommend that you buy sinkers, if only because sinkers (especially split-shot) tend to create long strings of lead-festooned fishing line, and when this stuff gets broken off it makes for ecological havoc down below. There are non-lead sinkers available, which is something to consider, although sinkers generally make things a little harder to manipulate, especially for neophytes, who often end up with a lot of line curled around their rods.

You might also want to buy a good old-fashioned bobber, one of those wooden cigar-shaped daubles that won't shatter on the rocks like the red-and-white plastic kind do. These are especially helpful for the young and/or inexperienced fisher, who might miss the tug of a fish's nibble but is likely to react to the sudden disappearance of the float. Bobbers facilitate a kind of hands-off fishing, allowing you to throttle Uncle Burl.

Mind you, no amount of tackle is going to guarantee that fish will be caught. Then again, neither does the presence of a $500-a-day guide armed with an underwater digital camera. (Oh, yeah, they got 'em.) So perhaps the most important angling equipment is patience and good humour. You might discover that your Uncle Burl is better company than you'd expected.

THE LORE OF THE LURE

I FIND nothing so pleasurable as finishing an evening meal up at Wolverine Lodge (an ancient hinterland hotel that several friends and I have pressed into operation as a kind of co-op cottage), walking out to the end of the dock and firing a fishing lure into the water. Granted, much of the pleasure derives from the fact that I am thereby absenting myself from dish-doing, but on some evenings—when the water is absolutely calm and the sunlight toes off the surface—there really is nothing I'd rather be doing. Except if you care to count actually catching a fish, because fishing with a lure is a dicey business, fraught with uncertainty and contradiction. A case in point: I once purchased a lure, a glowing green baby with fins like a '57 Chevy, designed to catch a huge, aggressive, pisciverous (don't worry, I'll get to it) specimen, such as the great northern pike. All I managed to catch was my buddy Jake in the forearm, but that's a whole other story. On the other hand, I was once angling for bait fish, trying to hook shiners with a minuscule golden hook and a shred of worm. Bang. I got hit by a pike. Go figure.

Everyone agrees that lures work, but as Dr. Ed Crossman puts it, "No one can conceive of why on earth they *do* work." This admission came as something of a shock to me, because if Dr. Crossman (the noted ichthyologist who wrote *Fishes of North America*) doesn't know, who does? "You might ask an angler," he suggested.

The trouble is, anglers haven't given the matter all that much thought. That is to say, their thoughts have been focused on specifics. Ask an angler "Why do lures work?" and you're likely to receive this sort of answer: "Because they're green," or "Because they're red and black," or "Because if you splash this baby down on top of the weeds late in the afternoon in the month of August, it drives 'em nuts."

We could begin by wondering how lures *might* work. Let's consider the nature and acuity of a fish's senses. The subject of sight is the obvious place to start, because some lures have been fashioned in slavish duplication of nature. This is especially true of flies, which have been tied with great entomological care. A Grey Wulff, for example, looks exactly like a mayfly, except it has a little hook protruding from its belly (and, if I tied it, is wearing a huge gummy turban of thread on its head). These lures are successful due to the manner in which trout (their primary designated target) feed. As mayflies hatch and emerge from the depths, to the surface and then into the air, the current pushes them downstream. This is like a conveyor belt of food, and trout sit in slower water (off to the side or in the eddy behind a rock) and nibble at their opportunistic pleasure. So the efficacy of a Grey Wulff lies not so much in its looking like a mayfly as in its not looking *unlike* a mayfly, if you see what I mean.

Most lures are designed to catch predatory pisciverous species, i.e., fishes that are hunting for fishes. Some therefore resemble the prey; they are shaped and coloured like a minnow or some other bait fish. (Like a perch, for example, which is not ethically, and in some regions not legally, a bait fish—it is a member of a target species—except many fish care naught for legality and ethics.) The most popular of such lures is the Rappala; the prototype was carved out of balsa wood and painted in realistic detail. It is important to realize that such lures would be fished near the surface. Although they now typically have plastic lips that force them downward, most are still spied, by the fish, from underneath. What the fish responds to is, therefore, a silhouette.

So, you might wonder, why not just toss in a stick with a couple of hooks stuck in it? From underneath a stick would possess the requisite minnowlike figure. And, indeed, there exists such a thing as a "stick bait," a dowel with hooks in it that merely lies on the surface. (The angler actually causes it to twitch, for reasons that shall become clear.) You might also wonder if the elaborate paint jobs are for the benefit of the fish or the angler.

For some time scientists bickered over the question of whether or not fish can see colour, but it now seems apparent that this is the case. "There have been some experiments which suggest that they are able to do so," acknowledges Dr. Crossman. "But what is painted on a lure is not necessarily what they see, because at depth much of the ambient light has been filtered out." This might explain the very odd tints and hues you find in a tackle shop. A pink or a blue lure, at depth, must possess, to the fish, a more natural sheen. I myself believe chartreuse to be a colour that, near the bottom of the lake or in water of considerable murkiness, has the ability to suggest to a fish, "Come on, eat me . . . you know you want to."

If your inclination is to fish with an artificial lure that imitates the prey, the secret lies in knowing what the local fish are eating. Is the primary bait fish the silvery shiner, or do the bigger fish tend to nibble on little perch, yellowy-greenish and slashed with stripes? Or does the water contain bass on the prowl for leeches or frogs? Replicas of both are available in the tackle shop, the frog-replicas being perforce more ornate than the leech-replicas. Once you embark on a stratagem of bait imitation, there seem to be no limits. I have seen a little plastic duckling, powered by a tiny paddle wheel, a bath toy with an evil gang hook dangling from the rear. After all, ducklings are delicacies for big fish like the muskellunge, so the deception makes a certain sense.

It is significant, however, that these types of lures—what we might call replicators—are often nowhere near as effective as lures that have no analogue in nature. What exactly is a Five of Diamonds imitating? For those of you who might be unacquainted, let me describe it. It is a "spoon" (actually, you should imagine a spoon with the handle cut away) rendered out of shiny silver metal, and on the convex back there is a pattern of five red diamonds. It is among the most popular lures in the world. How does it work?

There are, I think, two factors involved. One has to do with the subject we touched on above, colour. While it's true there are few fish marked by bright red diamonds, their darkness against the silver makes for sharp contrast. Contrast, in combination with movement, makes for what I'm going to term *flashing*. In the relatively static underwater world, flashing equals movement, and movement equals significance. In the little anecdote I cited above, wherein I caught a pike with a miniscule, barely adorned hook, I cunningly neglected to mention that just prior to the pike-bang the sunlight had glinted off the metal, making it shine momentarily like a jewel in the water. Another implication here is this: while anglers have their favourite colours, most would agree that it is a good idea to hedge your bets. Get at least *two* colours, so that the contrast (in combination with movement) gives you a bit of flashing. I even employ this philosophy when purchasing lead-headed jigs for still fishing, selecting ones that have been painted two disparate hues.

But all of the above is predicated on the assumption that a fish hunts mainly by sight. While this sense is definitely important to the fish, there is something else we have to consider: the lateral line system.

Dr. Brian Coad of the ichthyology department of the Canadian Museum of Nature notes that it's very hard to describe the lateral line system to a human being. "It's a sense that we don't have," he points out. "Basically it's like touch at a distance. It would be as if someone entered a room and, without seeing them or hearing them or anything like that, you'd just know they were there." So lures, by sending out vibrations through the water, alert the fish to their presence.

The nature of the vibrations is important. "There is a theory, for example," says Dr. Coad, "that sharks never want to eat human beings. But a human being swimming might register like a seal in distress." Which is to say, an erratic series of vibrations suggest to a fish that whatever is in the water is having difficulty getting about. Which is to say, injured. Which is to say, easy pickings.

Now we are getting close to a sound theory of how lures work. And I found the very man to voice it. Noel Alfonso is a fish biologist, a colleague of Dr. Coad's, but he is also a keen angler. Indeed, he guided at Great Bear Lake, an angling badge of some distinction. Here is his succinct summation: "Lures simulate the flashing, irregular movement of prey."

So now you can walk down to the end of your dock armed with scientific theory. First, you have to be reasonably certain there are piscivorous predatory fish in the vicinity: pike, bass or trout, for example. You should know what the fish typically feed on, so that you can approximate the prey's size and colouration. Make sure something about the lure flashes. It might be rendered out of metal; it might be bi- or tri-coloured so that there is contrast. And—here is where our knowledge of the lateral line plays in—make sure it *moves*.

Drag your lure near the dock so that you can see its action. A lure that swims surely through the water is not as likely to be effective as one that oscillates up and down or back and forth. I think highly of jointed, articulated lures, two halves linked together by a little swivel so that the bait sashays provocatively through the water. Vary your retrievals, i.e., reel in spurts and starts, jerking the lure. Try different speeds, looking for the one that pushes the "attack" button in the fish's brain. Oh, and by the way, we shouldn't disregard the fish's other senses. Many people scent their lures (there are various malodorous unguents commercially available), and though there is disagreement over whether the new smell is an attractant, it does mask human residue (insect repellent, that sort of thing.) A fish can hear, too, so it's worth investing in a couple of those lures with a little rattle inside.

Some beautiful gloaming when the water is still and the light is soft, try casting a lure off the end of your dock. And always remember this: you could be doing the dishes.

THE COMPLEAT ANGLER

HAD I horse's hair
and steel wrought by hammer—
Steel bent by wrench and
honed with whetstone—
a worm awakened
discovered under a turd
and impaled upon the point,
I would do no less well today.

Let me therefore consider the day.

FISHING WITH SANTA

THE Bow River is, by consensus, one of the finest trout rivers in the world, and for a period of six months I lived right beside it. Mind you, this was in the city of Calgary proper, and the Bow, as it ploughs through that Alberta metropolis, is fishable but stingy. Just south of the city, for fifty luscious miles, it is a generous river. But it is not the easiest water to fish. A big, determined river, the Bow has driven a deep furrow across the face of the planet. And it certainly isn't called the Bow because it meanders about; its name derives from the reeds that grow along its banks, which the Native peoples traditionally used to make bows. For the most part, then, it is not a good wading river, so the local fisherfolk have devised a nifty little vehicle—part bicycle, part paddle boat, part chaise longue—and they drift down the river in this, flogging the water and wheeling over to the bank for shorelunch.

I was very tempted to purchase one of these things, but I resisted: (a) because I didn't know where to fish, except very generally, like, *in the water,* and (b) because of the age-old river problem. The age-old river problem can be put very poetically: the river you step out of is not the same river you stepped into. That statement has much pith and is ripe for metaphorical pondering, but when discussing the Bow it has a more practical overtone: that is, the river you stepped into is soon about thirty miles away. So the owners of the little personalized river-wheelers have friends with little personalized river-wheelers, and someone drives to the put-in point and someone to the predetermined hauling-out point.

I didn't have a friend with one of those things; indeed, I only had one friend in Calgary who was even vaguely interested in fishing, and even then it was kind of a theoretical matter. Peter, the man's name is, had done little fishing and no fly-fishing, but he was attracted to the notion because he was on a bit of a Hemingway binge. Peter was inspired enough by "Big Two-Hearted River" to buy a fly rod, and I had given him some brief instruction on its use because there is a rumour, one I am not eager to dispel, that I actually know what I'm doing. But I will be truthful and admit that while I do indeed *know* what I'm doing, I am often not doing it. Wielding a fly rod requires great skill, and I have spent long hours trying to acquire it. I have gone so far as to cast competitively, although that experience ranks as one of the great humiliations of my life, and I've had more than my share of humiliations.

The point is, I couldn't ask Peter to buy a personalized river-wheeler, and I didn't know where we'd take the things, anyway, being Ontario-bred and new to the West, so my ruminations led to this conclusion: we needed a guide. I got on the Internet and searched for websites containing the words *Bow* and *River,* which led me to a site called "Bow River Anglers" and the words "My name is Barry White, the fly fisherman, and I have been guiding anglers on the Bow River out of Calgary, Alberta, Canada, since 1977." This had appeal because, well, I have to admit there was something pleasingly whimsical about the notion of fishing while a hulking man with a low-pitched growl exhorted me to make sweet, sweet love, and even though I was reasonably certain this wasn't *that* Barry White, I sent an e-mail and made an arrangement.

I invited Peter to come with me, my treat. This was a rare instance of largesse on my part (although it turned out to be diabolically clever, as shall be seen) because these Bow River guides aren't cheap. I probably could have bought a whole fleet of river-wheelers for the same money. But the guides charge what the market will bear, and that particular market will bear fabulously wealthy people from all over the world coming to test the waters. So I said to myself, "One only lives once," which is what I say in such situations, although I hope, deep down, that it isn't true. With that, on an early Saturday morning in early September, Peter and I drove to a certain tackle shop to meet our guide. Other anglers were also there to meet their guides, who started arriving in huge, chrome-bedecked four-by-fours, towing gleaming white dories. Soon everyone was gone, except for Peter and me. The clerk looked at us. "Who are you waiting for?"

"Barry White the fly fisherman," I responded, because that was how the man had referred to himself, and also because I wanted no confusion between him and Barry White the singer.

"Oh. Well, he'll be here."

By and by an awful sound filled the air, something akin to what Londoners must have heard on those dreaded nights of the Luftwaffe. This sound was produced by a pickup truck and seemed to announce its shuddering death throes, and when the truck pulled into a parking space it simply sputtered into non-ignition. A figure, obscured by the windshield but patently very, very large, fidgeted behind the steering wheel. *Hmm,* thought I, *maybe this is Barry White the singer.* But when the figure finally gathered energy and momentum and swung out of the cab, I had another, more definite thought: *Oh. It's Santa Claus.*

True, the figure was clad in clothes not associated with St. Nick—shorts, a T-shirt, sandals (or, at any rate, footwear that had begun life as sandals)—but in all other regards it was that cherry-cheeked man. He entered the tackle shop, looked at Peter and me and grinned impishly before leading us to the pickup. We climbed into the cab, sharing the seat with much detritus, and wheeled out of the city. I warily studied the man driving and said, "My name's Paul and my friend's name is Peter." I waited for a reaction; more precisely, I waited for a non-reaction, because if this man really was Santa, he would know that already, wouldn't he? Moreover, he'd know what we wanted in our heart of hearts and if we'd been bad or good. But he gave his name as "Barry" and asked if we'd fly-fished before.

"I've done some," I admitted. "Peter is a neophyte."

"Okay, Peter," he said. "I'll be keeping my eye on you."

NOW, in fairness, I guess I should clear this up. I know that the inclination runs contrary to much writerly wisdom, in that mystery is good fuel to keep readers reading, but here goes: this was not, in fact, Santa Claus. At least it was not the man who makes the yearly reindeer run, squeezing down our chimbleys. But the mistake was easy enough to make. Peter and I soon learned that Barry White the fly fisherman had two separate careers. In the summer, he guided anglers down the Bow River. In the winter, he returned to Edmonton where, for two years running, he'd been voted "Mall Santa of the Year." I could easily understand this. There was nothing phony about Barry's Claus-ness. The beard was real and long, the twinkle in his eyes was ever-present, and the girth was magnificent. This girth, I'll point out, apparently required regular maintenance; as we threw the gear into the dory, I realized that much of it was foodstuffs.

I suppose you might expect this story to proceed this way: Barry exhibited a manner at odds with his superficial St. Nickiness, cussing and spitting and what you will. That might make an amusing story, and I would be tempted to write it, except that it's not true. Oh, Barry smoked big Cuban cigars instead of a little briar pipe, but beyond that he was very Santa-like indeed, one of his most obvious characteristics (girth aside) being the propensity for gift-giving.

For example, standing there by the put-in spot, he watched briefly as Peter and I threaded leaders through guides with eye-crossing concentration. "Here, look," said Barry. He took the line and folded it where the leader was connected, and fed this more substantial entity through the guides. Then he tied on some flies for us. Peter pulled out line and tried to put the hook in the hook-holder, or at least what I think is a hook-holder—that mysterious little half-hoop of metal near the butt. "Try this," said Barry again, and then he showed us something fairly nifty, and if you pay attention here, you fly-fisher folk, you might learn a new trick. Barry fed out a substantial length of line, pulled this *behind* the reel so that it ran up the other side of the rod and then put the hook through a guide about halfway up. He cranked a bit so that this all tightened, rendering the ensemble easily transportable. "Then when you want to fish," he said, and gave the following demonstration. He yanked out some line from the reel and whacked down on the rod with a couple of fingers. The fly leapt out of the guide and fell away, leaving plenty of line free of the top guide.

"Hey," said I. "Neat trick."

We got into the riverboat, Barry oared away from the shore, and we were journeying down the Bow. Soon we came upon some fishing grounds, a straightaway studded with anglers standing chest-deep in the river, flogging the waters. Barry worked the paddles furiously and directed the boat over to the shore; he nestled the bow up onto the bank and worked some rope, dropping an anchor from the stern for security. Then it was into the river for Peter and me, armed with Barry's oral instruction in the art of nymphing.

According to Barry, one addresses the river and throws directly across it, or slightly upstream. The fly itself is weighted with little metal beads posing as bug eyes, and heads for the bottom. As things progress downstream, one mends line, turning circles with the rod as though it were a huge conductor's baton. When the line has reached its limit, the fly will rise from the bottom, and that is when fish are likely to be caught. You'll probably notice that I haven't mentioned what kind of flies were employed. I find that kind of detail needlessly cumbersome. Anyway, it's not as if I actually *knew* what kind of flies we used. We used whatever Barry tied on.

One thing about my casting is that it starts off fairly nicely but deteriorates rapidly. I mean, *really* rapidly, after maybe the first two or three casts. But off the top, on any particular day, I'm capable of capability. So it is that I managed to throw a couple of nice lengths, and Barry White said, "I'm impressed with your abilities, young man." There is, in my limited memory bank, a handful of wonderful sentences that people have spoken to me—"I love you," "It's a girl," "A little lower" (never mind about that)—and I immediately deposited this one: "I'm impressed with your abilities, young man." Peter didn't get off so easy, of course, because he was new to the game.

Here's the extent to which Peter didn't get off so easy: Barry actually *got out of the boat.* He did this with much gruntage, as it discommoded him immensely. Barry slowly made his way up along the bank, into the water, until he was standing beside Peter. Peter smiled meekly and, at Barry's urging, demonstrated his casting style. Our guide nodded, and his merry face jelled into something not quite so merry. He had his work cut out for him here.

"All right," he said, wrapping his own hand around Peter's on the butt of the rod. "Here's how we do it." I am familiar with various examples of imagery designed to illustrate the correct motion of a fly rod. Most typically, one refers to a huge imaginary timepiece, stopping the forward cast at eleven o'clock, the backward cast at one. But Barry's was more evocative. On the forward motion, he had Peter intone, "Hurl the hatchet." The chant for the back cast was more colourful still: "Stab the sky."

While all this was going on, yours truly took a fish. It was smallish, about a foot, a beautiful rainbow. I negotiated its capture (there was no battle, as such), eased the barbless hook out of its maw and settled it back into the river. Soon afterward, still buoyed by Barry's praise, I executed a fine cast that took my fly to the seam of some faster-moving water, and as soon as it hit I was tight to a much bigger fish, maybe six pounds. Oh, hell, seeing as I didn't catch it, I'm going to round off to ten. Then I took another, smaller fish and, well, let's just say that I was having big fun.

I CAN'T swear that Peter was also having big fun, exactly. Although Barry spent most of his time in the boat with his back turned away, he did indeed keep an eye on Peter, who was experiencing difficulties. Often Peter's line would get messed up, and he'd lose the fly on the shore behind him, or on his person, or somewhere in between. Barry was vastly experienced in the nuances of sounds. There would be a little snap, and Barry would say, "You lost your fly in a tree, Peter."

For his part, Peter was finding what little satisfaction he could in this sort of exchange.

Snap!

"I think you got the back of your vest, Peter."

"Hah! Wrong! That was my hat!"

When things got especially troublesome, when Peter was beyond flummoxed and flustered, Barry would (my friend came to dread this) abandon whatever he was doing and *get out of the boat*. It would take many long moments, sometimes minutes, for Barry to accomplish the journey from dory to fishing spot, time spent by Peter staring dolefully at the water, the fly line hanging limply by his side. "Let's go over this again," Barry would say. "Hurl the hatchet, stab the sky."

Now, I said that Barry would abandon whatever he was doing to help Peter. Some of you may be wondering what, exactly, he might have been doing. I myself was uncertain for a while. Barry was usually bent over, his hands in constant motion, and I thought initially that he might be tying flies streamside. I was impressed. It seemed like a keen thing for a guide to be doing—judging the hatch, the diet of the quarry, and then whipping up lifelike facsimiles. But Barry was not interested in the diet of the quarry. He was interested in his own.

Yep, he was eating. That's what he did most of the day. For lunch he brought sandwich makings (cold cuts, buns, onions, tomatoes, a blaster of mustard) and a big bag of chocolate cookies. Those cookies were tasty and high in calories, so every so often Peter and I, weary and needing energy, would go get one. We both thought the other was being mighty piggy, because the quantity of cookies diminished rapidly; we realized later that Barry, in fact, ate almost all of them.

Peter, I know, felt that he was being picked on. Barry would press the basics of fly casting upon him, often pulling the rod out of his hand to illustrate some aspect of the art. At one point I pulled Peter away to a shallow section of the river where we couldn't be overheard and tried to cheer him up. "Don't take it personally," I advised. I thought my friend was being a little thin-skinned, to tell the truth, because Barry's manner was very patient and friendly. "This guy knows what he's talking about. He's a very good caster, and there are fellows who spend hundreds of dollars to receive the education you're getting for free."

That was true enough: people do pony up huge wads of cash to learn how to fly-cast. But it was easy enough for me to be sanguine. For one thing, I was catching fish, lots of them. For another, the fact that Peter was receiving all this personal attention had a pleasing correlative: Barry was leaving me alone. That's why I mentioned earlier that my decision to invite Peter had diabolical overtones. I was being left alone. I could throw huge, ugly loops and get caught up and perform all manner of mis-fishing, and Barry was either eating or occupied with Peter.

At least that's how things stood until the wind picked up, at which point Barry turned his attention to me.

OKAY, one is addressing the river, perpendicular to it, and fly-casting. If one is right-handed, the line is in motion on that side of the body, correct? Yes. But if the wind is blowing from that side, then the line is in motion all over that side of the body, providing ample opportunity to get whipped, tweaked and hooked. There are several ways to combat this. One is to lower the rod from ninety degrees to, say, forty-five, so that the line is at a remove, but this increases the odds of getting caught up behind, because the fly is that much closer to the earth. With me, the odds of getting caught up behind are already pretty close to staggering, so that didn't seem the best way to combat the wind. I tried it, because I couldn't think of what else to do, but it was problematic. I gamely laboured on until I heard some huffing and puffing coming from behind me, at which point a clammy realization descended: Santa Claus is coming.

"All right," Barry said. "Let's see what we can do about this."

Many of you experienced fly fishermen know the techniques

I'm going to outline; then again, there really aren't all that many experienced fly fishermen out there. Mostly there are dilettantes (and I mean that in the best possible sense) like myself, who perhaps have not had to combat gale-force winds while fishing the Bow. There are a couple of things you can do. One is to throw crossbody, if you will, angling your forearm so that the line moves (I refer to the example above) on the left side of your body and gets gusted farther away. This, however, can affect accuracy (not that I was being much more accurate than trying to hit the river). Another option is to turn around. That's right, turn right around and throw toward the bank, in which case you lay down your back cast.

Uh-huh. That's what I said to Barry. I said, "Uh-huh."

He demonstrated, setting out a hundred feet of line on the water.

Wow. That's what I said. I said, "Wow."

Barry worked with me for an awfully long time, sharing an abundance of knowledge and skill. "Let's change the paradigm," he said at one point as I struggled with my lay-down. "There's no law that says you can't turn your wrist like this on the follow-through." He demonstrated, I copied, and although I never managed anything like the pokes he was capable of, I did end that day a better caster than I began it.

Which, come to think of it, was near the top of my list of what I wanted for Christmas—right after finding out where to fish the mighty Bow River.

BIG FISH

MY friend Jake is a Muskie Man.

Oh, sure, he'll fish with slathering glee for other species. But at fundament, he's a Muskie Man.

I first met Jake MacDonald perhaps ten years ago. I gave a reading in Kenora, Ontario, and thereafter encountered a handsome young man known variously as Chris, Cubby, Scout or Booger. (I tend to call him "Booger," although the sobriquet is not universally endorsed. For our purposes here, I'll just refer to him as "Cubby.")

Booger, oops, Cubby is a writer slash former Rowdy Lake fishing guide slash railroader, and with regard to that last post-slash, I will relate a little story that tells all you need to know about him.

As we talked that first evening, Cubby related that he'd been, for the past few months, working as the caboose guy. I immediately recalled my childhood, standing on a small hill, watching a train roll by; as the caboose passed, I would lift my hand and wave to the friendly fellow with his elbow on the sill of the little window. "Tell me, Cubby, do kids still wave at the caboose guy?"

"Oh, yeah. But you know kids these days," said the man

philosophically. "Sometimes you have to wave an awfully long time before they'll wave back."

Anyway, Cubby said there was this fellow I should meet, so the next day he picked me up at the hotel in his boat. (You have to know Kenora, Ontario, to understand how this works logistically.) We thence embarked on a thirty-five-mile journey up the Winnipeg River. Being a former Rowdy Lake fishing guide, Cubby had a number of rods in the boat, and periodically he would stop in a bay or something and say, "This is a good place to fish." As I cast, Cubby would survey the surroundings, and after a few minutes decide, "Okay, let's go." (He informed me only when we achieved our destination that in each of these instances he'd been lost.) The event from our journey that sticks out most in my mind occurred when Cubby needed to relieve himself. He spotted a smooth rock sloping out of the water and pushed his throttle forward, skittering the boat across the lichen-covered granite until it was unimpeachably beached. (That's nothing. Jake—whom you've yet to meet officially—told me that once he and Cubby were pickerel fishing late in the season. As they neared home—built upon the formidable Great Canadian Shield—Cubby, slowing down not a whit, turned to Jake and said, "Hold on. I'm putting her away for the winter.")

Our journey lasted all day, but finally Cubby and I came upon a wondrous sight, something from a fairy tale, or something that would be from a fairy tale if we Canadians had our own and didn't rely on those that take place in dense Germanic forests. Because

sitting on the water was a beautiful little house, an octagonal structure with a roof peaked like an elf's cap. "That's Jake's place," said
Cubby. A boat sat outside, a wooden boat that had been burnished
so that it glared and dazzled even in the dying sunlight. We pulled
up past this boat, caught hold of the planked walkway that encir-
cled the floating house. Cubby called Jake, and that man emerged
through the doorway.

My first impression was that Jake MacDonald was angry at
Cubby and me for interrupting his dinner. This was inaccurate,
chiefly because Jake doesn't really eat anything. He'll often
announce that it's time for dinner, breakfast, whatever, he'll prepare
the meal with enthusiasm and care, sit down behind the plate and
then shove the food around with his fork. It's as if the concept of
dining never really registered; instead of ingesting, Jake plays this
little game of platter hockey, flipping victuals about as he talks. No,
Jake was irritated that we'd interrupted his *dish-doing;* this is why he
held a fork in his hand and glared at us menacingly. His is the kind
of face that angries up very convincingly. He has sharp features,
set in a frame of deeply etched lines. And when he spoke—
"Booger . . ."—his voice rumbled forth wearing brass knuckles.

Jake has ankylosing spondylitis, a disease that, during his early
adolescence, fused many of his bones together. This doesn't slow
him down that much, but it gives him a distinctive stance, vaguely
ogrelike, I suppose, his arms always set at his sides as though
looking for rocks to hurl. So he cut an imposing figure there on

the dock/walkway, and my impulse was to flee, although Cubby was in charge of the transportation. He tied up the boat, leapt out and shook Jake's hand. "This is Paul Quarrington," he said.

Jake's expression, far from softening, darkened a few shades. "Come in," he said, and disappeared back into the floating house.

Jake and I went fishing together the next day, having discovered, over a few rounds of platter hockey and a bottle of single malt, that mutual passion. A few words about writers who fish: they make up a distinct subspecies of the literary set, and although I know many of them, I have actually angled with very few. David Adams Richards and I talk a great deal about fishing, but he favours the Maritime salmon rivers of his youth, and my journey to them has never been realized. I once spent a week in Saskatoon, the home of David Carpenter, and it looked, that time, as if we actually might make it out to the water. But he would daily come up with reasons why it wasn't a good idea (chiefly that it was too hot, not what you might expect in Saskabush), so, although Carp and I are both founding members of a touring assemblage called "Fishapaloosa," we have never actually wet lines together. But I've never had this problem with Jake, who early in our relationship demonstrated an ability to make things happen. That first time was rather easy: he gave me a place to sleep (basically right where I passed out) and then poured me into a boat the next morning. We fished for pickerel in a manner new to me, back-trolling into the current, hauling up lovely two- and three-pounders. I also caught a sauger, something I'd never done before. (A sauger is a smaller version of a pickerel and lacks the colouration; indeed, it seems to be a black-and-white photograph of a pickerel.) But over the years Jake's plans have become grander and grander, and we've managed to accomplish many of them. We've hammered the waters of western Ontario, we've fished the West Coast, we've journeyed to the Bahamas.

Somewhere along the line Jake's mood brightened, and when I imagine him now, it is with a grin carved into his face.

But like I said at the top, Jake is at fundament a Muskie Man, so what follows is a tale about the pursuit of that giant, first published in *Cottage Life*. David Zimmer, the magazine's editor, suggested that Jake and I fish together and then write about it without discussion, comparison or confirmation of fact. I think David wanted to see how boldly fishermen would lie even in print, but if so, his thinking was a bit misguided. An angler doesn't lie, in exactly the same manner a novelist doesn't lie, despite the fact that nothing he or she writes is true, exactly. Anglers only lie to *improve the narrative*, and as such are latter-day practitioners of an age-old oral narrative art form. So you will notice discrepancies and contradictions in the following tale. In it Jake and I both recount our first meeting, and you'll see these recountings are at odds, not only with each other, but with what you've just read. If you take all the versions and stir them up in a big pot, you get a soup that smells like the truth.

One more thing. I imagine that you might be a little bit baffled by the timeline that follows. I imagine that because I myself am totally flummoxed, and I was there. As close as I can reckon, we're talking about two full days of angling here; I was scheduled on the red-eye flight back to Toronto at the end of the second. And, to answer a question that you will no doubt raise as you finish the piece: yes, I boarded the airplane smelling like stewed fish entrails.

PAUL: The muskellunge is known as the "fish of ten thousand casts," an epithet that didn't really sink in until my arm was creaky, aflame with pain and noticeably thinner than the rest of my body. And at that point I still had nine thousand, eight hundred and twenty-two casts left to go. But aside from these physical problems (my back and shoulder-blade assembly would rattle and crack every time I raised the rod above my head), my life was at that moment very pleasant. I was in a fishing boat with my new friend Jake MacDonald.

Jake and I had been introduced to each other by Booger (the noted man of leisure and former Rowdy Lake fishing guide). Late one night Booger and I stepped, more than a little drunkenly, onto the dock surrounding a houseboat moored near the town of Minaki. The owner stepped out of the door, a deceptively frail-looking man with sunken cheeks and lively eyes. This man looked at me for a long moment and then said, "Hi."

It hardly rivals "Livingstone, I presume," but the meeting was fairly noteworthy. Two angler/novelists had finally encountered.

JAKE: I once saw a T-shirt that read EVERYONE HAS TO BELIEVE IN SOMETHING. AND I BELIEVE I'LL HAVE ANOTHER BEER. Fishing is the same sort of philosophical exercise. Once you get to a certain point in your life you realize, with a kind of vertiginous panic, that the sum total of your personal existence has about as much significance as a mosquito whacking the windscreen on a Kenworth. One glimpse at those big headlights and most people scramble for metaphysical straws. Some throw themselves into good works, poetry, travel or the pursuit of money. I prefer to go fishing.

The only drawback to fishing, as a lifetime diversion, is that it's hard to find someone to share the misery with. Because for much of the time, fishing is miserable. When the evening air is warm and the lake is stained with a gorgeous sunset, you can always find someone who'll tag along for a cruise. But what about those afternoons in the October freezing rain? Those brutally hot July afternoons when there's not a fish on the planet? Those endless hours of muskie casting with nothing but a case of tendonitis to show for it? The fact is, most people enjoy fishing only if the fish happen to be biting. If the fish are not biting, which is most of the time, the potential partners are few and far between.

One rainy, awful night, while doing the dishes and listening to the radio, I heard footsteps on the deck of the houseboat. Two sodden-looking men appeared at the door. One was my old friend Booger, the noted man of leisure and Rowdy Lake fishing guide.

The other was a stranger who wore glasses and an ill-fitting rain jacket and carried a muskie pole. "Jake," said Booger, "this is Paul Quarrington. He lives in Toronto, but he's visiting here for a few days and he's looking for somebody to go fishing with. And he doesn't care what the weather is like."

So that's how I met Paul. And although I felt pleased to have a new friend in my boat, I felt a certain amount of pressure to produce a big fish for his enjoyment. The first day, in drizzling rain, we cast heavy muskie lures all afternoon without seeing a fish. I tossed a foot-long vintage Pikie Minnow and Paul threw a Bermak, which is a futuristic-looking plastic thing that looks as if it should come equipped with a whip aerial and a remote control. We saw two muskies, but neither of them chomped our lures. By the end of the day, soaked, tired, stiff, we pulled up to the dock, and I asked Paul what he would like to do the next day. "Do you want to sleep in? Take a day off?"

I might as well have been Colonel Travis asking Davey Crockett if he had business elsewhere. "Tomorrow," said Paul, tipping his hat, "we fish."

PAUL: So it was now early morning and the new sun was burning the last licks of mist off the water. Jake and I were conducting a high-toned conversation about literature and film and their unnatural union, but that was but a pastime, and had nothing to do with our more profound occupation, trying to catch a *really large fish*.

I realize that this may not seem like the most worthwhile pursuit. I'm even willing to concede that the fisher of really large fish is standing on some fairly shaky ethical ground. But I don't care. We all have a tiny Captain Ahab in us, intent only upon the hunting down of the tiny Great White.

Mind you, when one still has nine thousand, eight hundred and eleven casts yet to make, one does start to think, *What right have I to bother these magnificent brutes?* Part of my difficulty lay in my selection of terminal tackle, the Bermak. Jake had pointed out this lure in the dockside sporting goods store, so I bought one. I didn't realize until later that Jake had pointed it out because he thought it looked ridiculous. It was moulded out of chartreuse plastic and looked very futuristic in a 1950s kind of way. The Bermak weighed about ten pounds and my best shot at nailing a muskie lay in landing the thing on a fish's head. Still, I had enormous faith in the Bermak, because one needs a totem or talisman when on such a quest. Plus, muskellunge lures seem to cost about twenty bucks apiece, so it's not as if I was about to buy another.

While I'm about detailing my problems, let me point out that every three or four casts, my reel would belch forth a Gordian knot of braided line. I'd swear inventively and hunch over the bait-casting reel, sheepishly deknitting the line. This was all the more embarrassing because I'd once been photographed holding bait-casting gear, a smug expression plastered across my face (insofar as that was possible, being as I had a cigar plugged into my mouth at the same time).

The image had been plastered across the cover of a literary journal, the sort of thing nobody reads—except, of course, for Jake MacDonald, who eyed me with deep suspicion.

At any rate, at some point around cast number two hundred and four (nine thousand, seven hundred and ninety-five left to go!), I made the following observation to Jake: "You know, Hemingway had a theory that as long as writers knew something totally, *absolutely*, then wha-wha-wha." Those of you who study Hemingway will realize that this was not his theory at all. I had been rendered insensible by the sight of the large duck-billed pike that followed the Bermak back to the boat. Jake had told me that under such circumstances one should describe a figure eight with the lure, hoping to provoke an attack, so I dutifully thrust my arm over the side of the boat, made something that vaguely resembled that number and watched the muskellunge continue by as if he was off to the paper box and had never been interested in the Bermak to begin with.

We flung our lures with increased vigour then and managed to raise the fish a couple more times, but on each occurrence he seemed to be running errands, and he did not chomp down on the Bermak, so Jake and I decided to try something different. We left Minaki, Ontario, and journeyed northwestward into Manitoba.

JAKE: The next day, charcoal-dark whitecaps crashed across the lake. Rain peppered our faces as we combed the islands and bays, looking for a fish so high and wild we'd never need to catch another. Some people call muskellunge "the fish of ten thousand casts." But I've figured out, from years of chasing them, that they're really "the fish of fifteen follows." After five fish follow your lure, the next one will strike. The trouble is, two out of three strikes result in lost fish. A little simple math showed that my goal of watching Paul catch a big fish was still a long way off.

PAUL: Jake had just written an article about the legendary catfish guide Stu Mackay, so he got on the phone and put into practice one of the more audacious capers I've ever heard, namely this: "Yeah, I've got my photographer here from Toronto. We thought if you had a couple of hours later this afternoon, we'd go out on the boat and try to get some shots." The audaciousness was evidenced by a question Jake asked as soon as he cradled the receiver. "Do you have a camera?"

"Well, yeah, sort of, you know, a little—"

"Good. Come on."

And that is how the two of us ended up on the Red River in a huge boat that resembled a landing craft from World War II. Nearby, tons of water cascaded over a concrete weir; boys with long fishing poles and torn nets played in the mist rising from it. It was raining. In point of fact, the Cloud Gods were running through their entire repertoire. "Besides the various types of actual rain," they cackled, "we have light drizzle, steady drizzle and, for the true connoisseur, *freezing drizzle!*"

We anchored and Jake threw out his line. Within seconds he was playing a catfish, *a large fish*. Stu Mackay was both cheering him on and casting suspicious glances at me. I was making my small plastic camera fire with all the fury I could muster, screaming, "Work with me, Jakey! I need to see it on your face!" My camera does have one or two little options that I thought might lend some semblance of professionalism. For instance, I could make the lens zoom in and out just by pressing a button, so I did that all the time, even if I was not at the moment preparing to make a photograph. Also, whenever a roll of film was completely exposed, the camera would rewind with a satisfying high-tech whirring sound, which I would try to enhance by spinning the instrument over my head by its strap.

I've no doubt we had Captain Mackay satisfied with our cover story. The only problem was that I was not doing any fishing myself, so I eventually announced, "I think I've got what we need," which I believe is something professional photographers actually say, and I took up a rod.

Those of you unacquainted with the lore of the Piscator may be missing an essential aspect of this piece: some anglers would feel that abandoning the muskie hunt in order to catch catfish is like passing up filet mignon in order to chew on frozen wieners, but I wish to dispute this. Our bait hung only a foot beneath the surface of the rain-bloated Red River, and there was a float attached to the line. I was told to keep close watch on that float, but I learned one thing about catfishing, namely, those guys don't bite unless you're looking away, unless you're talking to Jake or something, at which point there is a huge sucking sound and you feel your body impelled out of the boat into a huge vacuum. It is recommended that you stay inside the boat, of course, with your lower body squashed against the gunwales. The catfish will come to the surface, fuming like a punch-addled pug. It may lack the salmon's more acrobatic escape techniques, but the catfish compensates with infuriated thrashing, throwing his head back and forth with such muscular force that you almost get moved up and down in the boat. And with a salmon, you never worry that once you land the fish you might get beaten up.

Prevailing thought has it that catfish are not pleasant to look at. But the fishers of large fish, my friend Jake MacDonald and I, having managed through some grace to battle one or two to possession, slipped them back into the river and waxed profanely rhapsodic about their beauty.

JAKE: When the going gets weird, the weird turn pro. As I drove Paul toward Winnipeg, through the hardest rain in one hundred years of recorded weather, I remembered that some of the biggest fish in North America (channel catfish) live in the Red River. I also recalled that recently I'd happened to write a story about a fishing guide named Stu Mackay, the best catfish man in the Red River Valley. The editor needed a few glossies of Stu for the article, and the more I looked at Paul, the more he began to look like a professional photographer.

With great luck Stu Mackay happened to have a free evening, and in short order Paul, Stu and I were drifting down the Red River, wearing our cloth jackets and leather shoes in the downpour. For appearance's sake, Paul kept brandishing his tiny camera, making the lens zoom in and out, but soon he forgot all that as his bobber zipped under and his rod bent over from the weight of a very large catfish.

After an hour and a half, we'd boated and released a dozen giant catfish, and even Paul was soaked, hypothermic and ready to call it quits. Afterward, we stopped at a bar and ordered a couple of brandies. The waitress eyed Paul's muck-smeared cowboy boots, my taped-up hand, our rain-plastered hair, and wrinkled her nose at the dead-cat river smell rising from our table. "Where have you guys been?" she asked.

We both smiled. "Fishing."

MY MUSKIE CHERRY

ONE of the ways fisherfolk lie (I know I've stated that fisherfolk don't lie, but you didn't buy that, did you?) is numeri-
cally. As Samuel Clemens said, "There are lies, damn lies, and sta-
tistics," and although I don't know for a certainty that he was fin-
gering anglers, he might well have been. Here's what I'm getting at.
Suppose I were to spend a day upon the river, and over the course
of a few hours latch and dispatch several tiddlers, overambitious fry
with a mean length of, oh, six inches. At some point I take a
slightly larger fish, something approaching respectability, a full
foot. Now, that doesn't truly represent a big day (although like all
days spent fishing, it was likely very pleasant). But if, in summing
up, I report, "I took nine fish, the largest of which was thirteen
inches" (always round off *upward*), then things sound very fruitful
indeed. Sometimes, at the end of a day, a companion will assess
things arithmetically, and I myself am startled at the success we've
garnered. All I remember is catching a startled minnow and losing
a good rainbow, which both get mixed into the "fish taken" category. (Technically one is supposed to battle a fish to possession,

but since the creatures are slated for release, anyway, one can allow a certain latitude as to when that is accomplished. Therefore, anglers have conceptualized the LDR—long-distance release—which is very humane, as it involves no handling. In cowboy country, I learned about the *rodeo release*, which allows you to place a fish in the "taken" category if you've had it on your line for eight seconds.) Possessed of a foggy memory, I myself am not good at the numerical summation, so the report I am now going to give you, a report of a specific day spent on Lake of the Woods, was the computation of my longtime angling companion Jake MacDonald. Here it is: we raised eight muskies and took one.

That, as any muskie man will tell you, is one hell of a day, the order of outing one should expect only every decade or so. But if we examine it more closely, it diminishes in impressiveness. I might be reluctant to tell you about it at all, except that there was a very exciting episode, and Lord knows we could all use a little more excitement.

Jake and I journeyed from his floating house in Minaki to Kenora, Ontario, one morning in late June. We pulled into a supermarket parking lot with a boat ramp. That's the kind of town Kenora is: supermarket parking lots have boat ramps.

"There he is," said Jake, pointing toward the water, where a young man stood in a beautiful sleek boat, casting a muskie plug with the sort of carefree idleness that implies no great expectations. "That's Patrick."

Patrick looked toward us, nodded, gave us a two-fingered salute. He had taken off his shirt, and the process of saluting us set his upper body into rippling motion, making his right pectoral pop. What I'm getting at is, Patrick was well-built. He had obviously spent time in a gym, maybe most of his adult life. And this was certainly not the first time he'd ever peeled off his shirt, either, given the richness of his tan. Patrick wore a pair of wraparound sunglasses and had dark hair, densely curled. When he saw us, he moved to the steering console, threw the boat into motion and puttered over to the dock to fetch us.

From the drive down, I knew Jake's connection to this man, Patrick Nolan. Jake had a friend, Maxie, who was a Winnipeg police officer. This fellow, Patrick, was Maxie's boyfriend. They met on the job, Patrick being a paramedic. But Patrick was also eager to establish himself as a muskie guide, sharing the boat and expenses with another hopeful. And he was willing to take us out fishing, because Jake and I are outdoors writers and could enhance Patrick's reputation with a few well-chosen and -placed words. I might as well choose and place now: Patrick Nolan is a good guide. If you're ever out near Lake of the Woods, contact him at *patrick@sundanceguideservice.com*. There. Business out of the way. Let's go fishing.

I'm not sure how many of you are familiar with Lake of the Woods, but the salient fact for the nonce is that it's big. There are 65,000 miles of shoreline, making for a colossal oval of water that links up Ontario, Canada, and Minnesota, U.S. of A. This oval is studded, largely at the Canadian end of the oval, by something like 14,000 islands. As you set off from Kenora, the area is congested with cabins and cottages, some modest, some new and grand, some very old and grand. If there is a local in the boat, he or she will feel compelled to deliver the popular history: "And right over there is where Duke Wayne used to stay!"

Patrick wanted nothing to do with this civilization, and he tore away from it at fifty miles an hour (having abided all the NO WAKE signs, of course). The homes and hotels became less frequent, and eventually we were in the wilderness. The trip there was fairly long, giving us time to chat, if that name can be given to a conversational activity wherein words get yanked out of your mouth by the wind and tossed into the drink. Patrick reported a mishap that had occurred earlier in the week, somewhere on the huge lake; a bunch of fellows, friends of his, were goofing around on a dock, and one of them slipped and broke his leg.

"Who looked after him?" wondered Jake.

"I did," allowed Patrick.

"Did you know right away his leg was broken?"

"Oh, yeah. Classic case. Discolouration. Deformity." Patrick listed some diagnostic signposts. The fact that Patrick was a paramedic will have ramifications within these pages, so I wanted to remind you of it.

NOW, as to how I shall proceed. I've decided against using chronology as my organizational principle, because I'm not sure I can reconstruct the day that way. One of the reasons I like to fish is that it is not so much a pastime as a *changetime*, if you see what I'm getting at. A day spent fishing is characterized by moments, yanked out of the quotidian and scattered across the water, which my memory then reassembles according to brilliance and remarkability. So I will link each of the fish to a moment, eight in all. Also, if I were to record the day according to the tyranny of the timepiece, the exciting bit would come fairly early on. And after all these years, I've learned enough about the craft of writing to become, well, crafty.

I shall also attempt to categorize many of the muskies. For example:

1) The Mugger

Jake was fishing from the stern, nestling his hip against the housing of the outboard motor. He is a good caster and concentrated on landing his huge, hairy lure near the shoreline, some hundred feet away. As he retrieved, Jake scanned the water, looking for trailing shadows. Thus, he was not expecting the mugger muskie, who was hiding behind the outboard motor and appeared in front of the bait just as Jake was about to bring it into the boat. The fish (I was witness to this) appeared so suddenly that it seemed its objective was to startle rather than attack. "Aha!" the muskie shouted silently. "Give me your wallet and your watch!" This was a big boy, too, so beefy that I suspected it had spent time working out with Patrick, the two of them spotting each other on the bench. Jake was in the process of hoisting his bait, so he had to do two things immediately, sooner than immediately. First, he had to drive his rod tip down into the water and make the lure turn the figure eight that sometimes provokes an attack. Second, he had to suffer the massive coronary that accompanies the sudden manifestation of a big muskie. But the fish was gone, maybe recognizing Patrick and knowing that the man had ties to the police.

2) "Did You See That One?"

"Did you see that one?" asked Patrick, nodding toward my lure.

"That one what?"

"That fish."

"There was a fish?"

"Yeah. A good one, maybe twenty-five pounds."

"Oh?"

"He was pretty interested. You should have done the figure eights by the side of the boat."

"Oh."

"Next time," said Patrick, smiling, although whatever gods govern fishing were giving no assurances that there would be a next time.

I'm not very good at seeing fish in the water. You may have gathered that by now, but I wanted to broach the subject with candour. Over the years I have invested several thousand dollars in Polaroid sunglasses. Sometimes there are little sales devices in the optometrists' shops, small murky photographs that become clear with the donning of the lenses and reveal hidden beauties. So I buy the sunglasses, take them out upon the water, don them with great hope in my heart and peer down and see, um, nothing. I recall stories about ancient Native fishermen who—without Polaroids—could discern great detail, individual pebbles at the bottom of a fast-moving river. Our guide Patrick was Native, you know, from the Ojibway nation, which may be significant. Also, he had sunglasses, pretty fancy ones, so I didn't feel too bad when he said, "Did you see that one?"

3) The Modern Muskie

Angst-ridden and existentially hobbled, the modern muskie evidenced a failure to commit. Patrick was retrieving his bait when the fish appeared, shooting from the shadows, its maw agape. Patrick braced and waited, and when he was confident that the beast had clamped down, Patrick set the hook and *ploop*, the hook came shooting up into the air. He didn't cuss, not right then, because he had to redeliver the lure and turn the figure eights, but the fish was gone.

Then did Patrick cuss.

4) and 5) The Synchronized Swimmers

These two hid in the weeds and waited, I think, side by side, until such time as two lures hit the water simultaneously. Then one said, "And a-one, and a-two, I'm on the left, the right's for you," and they cruised out, followed the baits for a few moments, each keeping a distance of a yard and a half. Then—I missed the cue, it must have been very subtle indeed, the merest wiggling of a fin—they veered off and swam back to the shadows where they awaited the judges' scores.

6) The Rocket

This was the grandest fish of the day, and here indeed is a moment marked by remarkability. Patrick tossed his lure, began to crank it back toward the boat. A huge muskie, behaving with patent ferocity, sped toward the thing asnappin'.

The fish missed the bait.

I am not an experienced muskie angler, so my observations are not to be given too much credence, but it seems to me muskies often have this combination of characteristics: they are ferocious, and they are myopic. Or perhaps when they are ferocious, when the instinct to kill fuels them, their vision is clouded by blood or adrenaline or passion. Anyway, this one's was; he just plain missed. Patrick continued cranking, hoping that the fish would attempt to redress the error, but the fish did not. Instead—and neither Patrick nor Jake, experienced muskie men both, had ever seen anything like this—the fish waited a moment and then rocketed into the sky. It came straight up out of the water and continued until its tail broke free. Four feet of pissed-off fish stayed suspended in the air for a magical moment, and then it keeled over sideways, smacked the water and was gone.

7) Sorry, I Wasn't Paying Attention
Sorry, I wasn't paying attention.

8) My Muskie Cherry
All right, so here, finally, Quarrington breaks his Muskie cherry. And he does it in Quarrington style, too. I cast my lure and bang! Er, let me rephrase. I cast my lure and bang!

I said to Patrick, "Um . . . "

"You got a fish!"

"Really?"

"Yeah, yeah, reel it in."

I reeled whilst in the waters behind the muskie battled with determined frenzy. But I emerged victorious, on account of my being a fine angler and on account of this muskie only weighing three pounds. It was netted and the hook extracted. Jake insisted on taking a photograph of me, Patrick and the fish. "All right, Paulsie," said Jake, "hold it out there, turn it a bit . . ."

"Hurry up, Jake," said Patrick. "Something's wrong with this fish."

"Okay, okay." Jake triggered the shutter. "Just one more."

"No," said Patrick, not that he was at all a disagreeable fellow. But there was great concern and worry in his voice. He flew to the side of the boat, and with a hand supporting both fore and aft of my fish, lowered the muskie into the water. He released it. The fish didn't go anywhere. Patrick began to move the fish so that water would flow through its gills. Nothing. He got out a muskie cradle so that the fish could be held more gently, attended to it by the side of the boat. Patrick the paramedic continued his ministrations for fully twenty minutes, and I half expected him to try mouth-to-mouth, maybe even to haul out those paddles, rub them together and holler, "Clear!"

I am more than convinced that Patrick did everything he could. But the fish died.

And, yes, I feel bad that the fish died, and perhaps that has murked up my memories of what was in many ways a wonderful day.

But let me return to my theme, which was how an angler often uses numbers to enhance an account of a fishing expedition. My buddy Jake is a master at this, and as we drove back toward Kenora, late that afternoon, he demonstrated his unique genius in an attempt to make me feel a bit better about my muskie cherry.

"You know," he said, "the average muskie in this lake is seventeen pounds."

"Yeah?"

"So, when you think about it, a three-pound fish is as unusual as a forty-pound fish."

I thought about it, nodded without comment. I have now caught a muskie; perhaps I will fish for them no more.

THE RETURN

A FEW *years back, I wrote a book called* Fishing with My Old Guy. *If you are enjoying this book, you might enjoy that one also. It detailed a trip that four men made (I should know, because I was one of them) into the extreme, way up there in northern Quebec. Gordon, Paulo, Gary and I were in search of the world's biggest speckled trout. Scientists say that such a fish is likely to live in one of two places: northern Quebec or Argentina. When I give public readings from* Fishing with My Old Guy, *I do not disclose whether or not the great beast was taken. (The Publisher advised this policy.) I do, however, tell the assembled that I am working on the book's sequel,* Fishing with My Old Guy in Argentina.

Some time after that adventure I returned with my Old Guy to the extreme. We had a couple of different companions this time, Rick and Paul. We caught fish, some of them pretty hefty, but nothing slated for the record books. The first trip had been scuppered by bad weather, and plenty of it. This time around things were beautiful, maybe even too much so, because someone concluded, "It's too warm for the big fish to start moving."

The Publisher was expecting another volume, but I knew I was in trouble. "Guys," I complained, "I can't write one book where the weather's too horrible and then another where it's too nice."

Then I had a little inspiration. When I got back to Toronto, I phoned up the Publisher in Vancouver. "We had a great trip," I told him.

"Is there a book in it?"

"Not a book," I said, "A poem. A grand epic poem."

I fully expected the Publisher to ring off abruptly, thereby releasing me from any obligations. But being the Publisher, he was silent for only a moment. "That could be good," he judged.

"I said a poem."

"Excellent," said the Publisher, who is a man of enthusiasms. "When will you be finished?"

You will see that my piece is hardly an epic, and it might not even be a poem. But I hope it conveys some sense of our journey.

The End of Canada

1.

We went to the end of Canada:

By foot to our cars
From our homes
Filled with loved and little ones
By our cars to Gordon's
Home where Sheila watched us
Load provender into the land shark,
Into the trailer with its tiny
Wheels
And its greasy tarpaulin.

By land shark to the highway
That connects upper to lower Canada
By highway to Montreal
By Montreal to night
By dawn to Chibougamou.

We were not at the end of Canada.

2.

We went to the end of Canada:

Clouds had settled in.
Because the clouds could not fly,
They ate dinner in a buffet restaurant
That served frogs' legs and giant prawns
And then the clouds went to a motel room
Where they slept two to a bed
In a double room.

They all masturbated and went to sleep.

They were not at the end of Canada.

3.
We went to the end of Canada.

We went in an airplane that had been designed
By Leonardo da Vinci,
Drawn on a piece of parchment
With chalk that Leo had dug out of the earth himself,
Thereby blackening his nails forever.

The pilot knew nothing of this.
The pilot sat with huge foam mouse ears on his head
Every so often he would pick up the radio transmitter,
And speak in a foreign tongue.

Electricity would answer.

Electricity would report that
Storms claimed the welkin,
And although we were welcome to the land,
Electricity could not guarantee safe passage.

That was all right for we four,
We who wanted to go to the end of Canada.

4.

We wanted to go to the end of Canada.

One was young and lean and smoked cigarettes.
One was a little older, a little meatier, and didn't.
I was older still, much meatier, and I smoked cigars
And also the young man's cigarettes
Every so often.

The fourth man was the oldest.
He had been to the end of Canada

Before

When he was young. When he was a young man
He went to the end of Canada.
He fished at the end of Canada
And caught a fish of such brilliant hue that he went
Blind, in a way.
Although he could still see,
He could only see certain things
And then only when the sunlight glanced off them
Just so

Or if they were hidden behind waterfalls
Or buried in the earth beside poisonous mushrooms.

It was to get his sight back—
It was to go blind forever

That he went to the end of Canada.

5.

Up the river by canoe.

The trees that stood by the river were naked
They were black and shrivelled burn victims
Fires had burned the edges of Canada.

And overhead, where God,
Wearing the old cotton shirt that He never takes off—
Not even for company—
Overhead there was fearsome energy.

Storms waited at the end of Canada,
Thuggish storms, still angry
Over some misunderstanding

That happened years and years ago,
Years and years before the end of Canada.

6.

In the river an island waited for us,
And had been waiting for what seemed like ever,

The island had passed its time
Doing watercolours

Although the island's technique had improved
Over eternity

The island's subject matter had grown
Banal.

7.

The men made their camp and went to sleep
And in their sleep fishing dreams came.

Fishing dreams come to men,
Just as running dreams come to wolves

Or walking dreams to fish.

So fishing dreams come to men
Especially when they are near the end of Canada.

8.

They awoke and climbed into canoes.

The river was pissed at them for being
Awake so early . . .
So it roiled and bubbled and bounced them
Rudely over rocks.

The river didn't care.

Sometimes it made two of them walk
Along the cling of the bank
While the old man and another
Rode the dare
With the old man in the stern
Hooting like an owl with a shillelagh up its arse
The other leaning out over the bow
Waiting for something to be stuck up his own.

The river didn't care.

Sometimes the river made them *all* get out,
The river made them bind the boat

With rope, fore and aft,
And lead the canoe like slaughtermen lead
Cows to the hammer,
Bucking and bulky and hard to handle.

The river didn't care.

The river laughed.

But they were almost at the end of Canada.

9.
Right before the end of Canada
The very second, the instant before
Was an island.

It was the most wonderful island
Because there were beautiful fish made of gold
In the water all around it

And peanut butter sandwiches grew on the little bushes there.

The peanut butter was chunky and the fish were fat.

The men all ate and grew stronger;

Then they paddled
The last few moments
Across
To the
End of Canada.

10.

There was a waterfall at the end of Canada.
Beside it was a stream.
The stream tried to be like its big brother,
But it was just a stream, not a waterfall.

We began to walk alongside it.

And the fish saw us and waved

And the fish said,
"Psst, buddy, want to see a picture of my sister?"

But we kept walking and then

We were there.

11.

And at the very end of Canada
There was a pool.
I dropped a Despair through a cloud of black flies
And it was taken
With a sound light as a kiss—
But no kind of kiss that you or I
Have ever given or received—
And at the end of the line was a brook trout
That weighed two perfect pounds.

12.

And then I turned away
And Canada
Went on forever.

BONEFISH ANSIL

"WHERE is he?"

That is what my friend Jake said to me, although he knew I didn't know, because I had asked the same question just a few minutes before. That is about all we were doing, exchanging that query. The setting was nice enough. We were in a marina on Bimini, the most westerly of the Bahamas, so small on most maps that it's virtually invisible. We were fishing Ernest Hemingway's haunts, because this island constituted one of the points on his Caribbean angling triangle: Key West, Cuba, Bimini. And no, we weren't waiting for Papa to show up, although the house he used to live in was just up a little hill. Even if he had been alive, it was too early in the day. Papa would still be working on his daily quota, 500 words. Then again, the sun was popping high into the sky, and any minute now Hemingway might descend the hill, sweaty and bumptious and eager for a drink. (Had he been alive, as I say.)

My point is, it was getting damned late (I can't mention Hemingway without calling something *damned*), and our fishing guide, Ansil "Bonefish" Saunders, was nowhere to be seen.

Hiring a fishing guide is, almost always, a good idea, but when hunting bonefish, it's a no-brainer. Because bonefish do have to be *hunted*, you know, they must be stalked. What happens is this: during high tide, the creatures move up onto the flats in order to feed. They eat off the bottom, inclining themselves so that, if the water levels are right, the tips of their tails can be seen above water. Even a sort such as myself, moving through life more than a little oblivious to things, can see when this tailing is going on. But often the bonefish remain totally submerged, and this is problematic for the angler, because the fish are silver to the point of mirrorishness, reflecting their sandy surroundings, and the only clue to their existence is shadow, a darkness in the watery panorama that requires great skill to discern.

This is the guide's first function: to scan the waters and to announce, "Bonefish." The client reacts to the statement with a stiffening alertness, a readying of equipment, a whispered "Where?" The guide—speaking very quietly, for these are timorous beasties—refers to a giant imaginary timepiece. "Two o'clock." The client peers through his Polaroids and, if the client is I, asks for additional information. "How far away?" "Fifty feet, sir." Then the bait is thrown. Conventional tackle is wielded with some delicacy; any sort of plopping will make the bonefish disappear, instantly, almost magically. And if one is using a fly rod, the casting must be done quickly and with a minimum, ideally an absence, of falsecasting, because bonefish, after millennia of predation at the hands, the talons, of seabirds, are ever wary of attack from the sky.

If this sounds tricky, that's because it is, and that is why only a very experienced bonefisher would attempt it without a guide. And the guide owns the skiff, you know. This is a certain kind of boat, designed so as to draw very little water, therefore capable of roaring about on the flats. When it's time to fish, the guide cuts the motor and climbs up onto a platform surmounting the engine housing. The guide takes up a long pole and begins pushing the craft through the mangroves, turning his head slowly from side to side, always watching.

Of course, I only knew all this from angling magazines. I'd never been bonefishing before; neither had Jake. Which accounted for our restlessness and our repetition of the phrase, "Where is he?"

We had long ago grown bored of watching the ongoing activity at the marina, although some of it, at least initially, was damned interesting. (Sorry, sorry, I'll try to curb that impulse.) For example, two young men had earlier loaded up some enormous coolers with ice. They put these into a small runabout, which had motored out to a large sportfishing vessel. The runabout was hoisted up at the stern of the sportfishing craft, which had thence ploughed through the swells to a huge yacht, surely over a hundred feet long. The sportfishing vessel was hoisted up at the stern of the yacht, and the yacht began to move away, and I imagined that somewhere out on the ocean was a colossal Mothership waiting to receive it, and who knew where this was going to all end? Oh, my, there was money evident on the isle of Bimini. Jake and I had precious little of it, mind you, although we were behaving as though we were rich international playboys, engaging the services of the island's most famous fishing guide. But we had cut a deal. Jake was profiling Bonefish Ansil for a magazine, so the guide had decreased his fee considerably. I was writing no magazine article, but was posing as Jake's photographer, a ruse we had worked in the past. We had worked the ruse very successfully, considering I had precious little photographic expertise, nor in this case, come to think of it, a camera.

"Maybe I'll go buy one of those disposable cameras," I announced.

"I'll wait here in case the guide shows up," said Jake.

So I toddled off down the street of the town. I would say the *streets* of the town, except there was only one, a winding cobble-stoned affair with water standing in it two inches deep, water left over from a hurricane that had battered the town a couple of days before our arrival. Bimini at its widest is only 700 feet across (and seven miles long), so it couldn't really accommodate more than the one street. I walked along it, dodging the golf carts that the locals used as transportation.

There was a small store (and when I say *small*, I mean I had to turn sideways to enter it) that catered to touristy needs. The stock in trade was seashells, but I did spy, up near the antique cash register, a little disposable camera, so I effected that purchase, making the transaction with a woman who managed to be pleasant without speaking a word. Then, as I was leaving, a man reared out of the shadows.

He had been sitting in a lawn chair in the corner, and he had been sitting so still that I truly had not noticed him until he made this action. I thought he must be store security or something, so I proffered my receipt.

The man asked, "Did you want to go fishing?"

"No," I said. "I mean, yes. But, I mean, we *are* going fishing. My friend and I. We're waiting for our guide."

"*I'm* your guide," he explained with grudging patience.

Because I had no response to this (or rather, was politely stifling the logical, "What the hell are you doing in *here?*"), the man pointed to his heart, to the material covering it, where stitching announced: ANSIL SAUNDERS. BONEFISH LEGEND. WORLD RECORD 16 POUNDS.

"Oh! Well, it's very nice to meet you, Mr. Saunders. My friend and I—"

"Meet me at the dock," he snapped.

And then the man was gone, flying out of the store with such propulsion that it seemed as though a little lick of gale-force wind, left over from the storm, had kicked him in the ass.

I hurried along to the dock, where my friend Jake was stuffed inside the telephone booth. (We had spent some of our waiting time trying to make contact with friends and loved ones, and then had moved on to friends and liked ones, and I suspected that Jake was now seeing if he could locate old high-school flames and such.) I kicked upon the Plexiglas and exclaimed, "He's coming, he's coming!" I know that many writers eschew the verb *exclaim,* but that's really what I did, as Ansil's bristliness had instilled a kind of urgency into the proceedings.

We waited at the dock—for quite a little while—and finally Ansil appeared in his beautiful boat. However, Jake's innards had, just previous to this event, told him to visit the commode, and Ansil became irritated. "Where's your friend? We don't have all day."

When Jake emerged, Ansil reiterated that fact, that we didn't have all day, and Jake's face clouded and he muttered something about Ansil having wasted most of it. Ansil demanded, "What was that?" and Jake went surly and silent.

Now, the client relies upon the guide's expertise and instruction, and Ansil was willing to provide this. However, he seemed to think it was his role to instruct us in all manner of things, for example:

"Climb down that ladder backward!"

Or . . .

"Sit down there! Move forward a bit! Move over to the right! Put your hands on your laps!" Well, maybe he didn't tell us where to put our hands; then again, they were already in our laps, folded together in meek supplication.

"All right. Let's go fishing."

We roared away in the beautiful boat.

I will say a few words about this boat, or rather, I will refer to Jake's reportage. Jake is the keener when it comes to boats (he himself has refitted a lovely old Peterborough), and all of this information comes from his interviewing, although for the most part Ansil offered up information rather stingily. So then, in Jake's words:

> In addition to being a fishing guide, Saunders is also a master wooden boat builder, and when he came to pick us up at the dock in Bimini, he was driving an exquisite wooden skiff that he built himself. The boat has oak ribs, gleaming mahogany floor boards, and knee braces carved from a hard, extremely tough local Bimini wood called "horseflesh," a kind of mahogany. His skiffs work well on the flats, and they're so beautiful that they've been displayed as "boat art" at large sports shows in Florida.

Now, I am an aesthetic creature, and I could appreciate the boat's beauty, but that's not the reason I have supplied the information. I did so that you might understand the annoyance Ansil felt with me because, in the busyness of loading the skiff, I had failed to notice that a single grain of sand had affixed itself to my sandal and was marring—*marring*, I say—the beautiful burgundy finish.

"Don't you know anything about wooden boats?"

"No, I don't know anything," I said, my voice dripping with something. Sarcasm, maybe. At any rate, it was dripping with a rhetorical nuance that failed to register with Bonefish Ansil. "You'd better learn something," he advised me sternly.

There was a passage through a mangrove, um, grove. (Unless there was a grove through the *mans*, and the word *mangrove* is a kind of portmanteau.) On either side of us the trees stood, all gnarled and twisted like leprous supplicants. Ansil roared through, but he turned his head from side to side, and at one point gesticulated with the hand that was free of the tiller. "You know," he called out over the engine's hum, "I wrote the hundred and fifty-second sam!"

"What?"

Bonefish Ansil offered no clarification. He nodded at the scenery we were screaming through. Saunders seemed, in some very vague way, to want Jake and me to appreciate how beautiful it all was. From time to time, as he rounded a corner, Ansil would steer his craft extremely close to the foliage, as though he wanted us to appreciate how beautiful it all *smelt*.

Then the passageway opened up onto the flats. Bonefish cut the engine, picked up his staff and began poling. He did this for a long time, saying nothing; and because I did nothing during this long time, other than look at Ansil Saunders, this seems a fitting time to describe him physically.

He was, undeniably, a very handsome man, chiselled out of black stone when the Creator was pretending to be Michelangelo. Ansil was all muscle, sinew and perfect proportion. And the years seemed not to have touched him; although I knew from Jake's research that he was in his late sixties, Ansil looked much younger. I suspected that even Time was intimidated by the Bonefish Legend. Time had probably turned away muttering, "I'm not going anywhere near that crusty bastard."

"Get in the water."

"Beg your pardon, Mr. Saunders?"

"Get in the water! In the water. *Get in!*"

Jake and I slipped over the gunwales.

Saunders pointed in a certain direction and told us, "There's bonefish over there! All sorts of bonefish!" He then took two fishing rods, long poles outfitted with spin-casting gear. He worked on the terminal tackle, fixing live shrimp over the hooks. Ansil handed us each a fishing rod and commanded, "Go!"

"But—" I began, but then fell silent, for I am at base a great coward.

"We've never fished for bonefish before," finished Jake.

Bonefish Ansil very decently contained the rage that threatened to blow the eyeballs out of his skull. "Throw the shrimp at them," he explained. "Catch 'em!"

"Okay, okay, okay."

We turned and began to walk in the *exact* direction Ansil had indicated—

"Not there! Over *there!*"

Okay. We corrected and began to walk in the *exact* direction—

"Over *there!*"

There is a little trick God pulls every now and again. When you first try something, God pulls out all the stops, creates extraordinary circumstances and rewards you with great good fortune. We have come to understand this as "beginner's luck," but it really is a much more insidious thing, a nastier prank, because you wander away with that event imbedded in your mind as the norm, and you are thereby doomed to a life of disappointment and failure. I mean to have a little talk with God about this at the first available opportunity, because He has done it to me many, many times.

This was one of them. As Jake and I waded forward, we began to see that, many yards distant, the surface of the water was rippling. And moving closer still, we could see little metallic flashes, tiny silver wedges that glinted in the sunlight. Bonefish, lots of them, were tailing, that is, eating from the bottom, inclining themselves so that their nether tips broke the skin of the water. We stopped in our tracks and watched for a long moment. Then, slowly, we prepared to cast. "You go for the left, I'll go for the right," suggested Jake, and we threw our bait near the fish. There was a fat moment during which nothing happened. Then it seemed as though my bait, the shrimp itself, made a break for it, scampering off for the horizon. I hadn't felt a pickup, but line was disappearing from the spool, so I set the hook. That didn't seem to accomplish much—there was no halting, no furied fishy leap or anything—but I had every reason to believe I was fighting a fish. Or rather, I was *engaged* with a fish, because there was little sense of battle. Line was vanishing from my reel, and though I lifted my rod tip heavenward, line continued to do so.

Jake, I might mention, was having the same experience.

Bonefish can, and do, often simply keep going. The angler looks down at his little spool and watches the final wrappings evaporate and he glimpses fleetingly the pitiful knot, the dumb little double cross hitch, and it goes *plip* and the fish is lost forever. But Physics can often lend a hand. (Part of the reason I love fishing so much is that I like having Physics as a fishing buddy, all got up in old clothes and willing to get his hands dirty.) What I'm getting at is that all that line out, given the accumulated water pressure, can dissuade the bonefish, and the creature will slow, stop momentarily and then head right back for the boat. It then becomes necessary to crank like a madman. The handle seems to diminish in size with each turn, and it becomes harder and harder to hold on to, especially given the pain that has cramped the hand muscles, the sweat that has slicked the plastic. Again, there is no clear reason for the fish to stop this activity, and sometimes it doesn't, continuing right on underneath the boat and recommencing the furious unspooling. But bonefish seem to be unusually game beasties, and near the boat they will flip out of the water and issue a silent challenge: *Give it your best shot, sucker.* With some skill and a large element of luck, the angler will win the day.

That is what happened to both Jake and me. We managed to catch these bonefish. Jake took my photograph, and then I took Jake's.

"No, not like that!" said Bonefish Ansil. "Get over there! Get over there, get the sun behind you there, and you, hold that fish up high, no, higher than that, okay, now . . . what kind of camera is that, anyway? Seems like sort of a cheap camera for a photographer to have."

Having had that initial and thrilling little bout with the quarry, we proceeded to hunt them with no great success. Ansil was quiet and withdrawn—which we counted as a good thing—except that every so often he would announce that he'd written the hundred and fifty-second sam. "I used to think that I'd written the hundred and fifty-*first* sam," he muttered. "But then they found one that had been written in the desert. So I've written the hundred and fifty-*second* sam."

"Right."

"It's a good sam."

"Anything you say, Mr. Saunders."

But eventually boredom brought with it the inclination toward conversation, even if that impulse seemed doomed from the outset, and Jake and I began asking questions.

"Who was the most famous person you've ever taken out?"

"Dr. Martin Luther King, Jr."

"You took Martin Luther King *fishing?*"

"No. He didn't want to fish. He wanted to *think*."

"Uh-huh."

"So I took him to the place where I wrote the hundred and fifty-second sam."

Now, there's no reason why you should have to wheedle this story out as Jake and I did, so I'll summarize on behalf of Bonefish Ansil. Former congressman and civil-rights leader Adam Clayton Powell was a longtime visitor to Bimini, familiar with the locals, so when his friend Dr. King bemoaned the fact that he needed to write an important speech but lacked the quietude to do so, Powell had a suggestion: come down to Bimini. There, Dr. King was hooked up with Ansil Saunders, who listened to the problem and knew just what to do. He sat Dr. King in his boat and motored out to the grove of mans. He cut the motor at a certain spot and indicated the surroundings. "That," said Saunders, "is where I wrote the hundred and fifty-second sam."

I'm sure Dr. King was quicker on the uptake, but it was only around here in the telling that Jake and I received elucidation. "Ah," we said, almost as one, "the hundred and fifty-second *psalm*."

"That's what I said, *sam.*"

"Right."

The speech Dr. King was working on was his acceptance of the Nobel Peace Prize in 1964. In it he outlines the problems facing humankind, many of which have arisen from technology, humankind's clumsy manipulation and, indeed, Dr. King does seem to have been reminded, for some reason, of the natural world: "We have learned to fly the air like birds and swim the sea like fish, but we have not learned the simple art of living together as brothers."

I wouldn't say that Bonefish Ansil implied he'd co-written the speech (although I don't think he would offer any blanket denials, either), but he did tell us that when Dr. King arrived he had not been a well man, beset by worriments and woes. "So I took him to the place where I wrote the sam," said Ansil. "I tied the boat up and we sat there for two hours, looking at the clouds, the sky, the little fishes moving in the water, and when we left he had tears in his eyes, because he was so moved by the beauty of this place."

Bonefish Ansil put us on a couple of bonefish then, to which Jake and I miscast. Surprisingly Saunders didn't seem to care all that much; by that point in the day, Jake and I had each brought two fish to uneasy submission, and our guide seemed to think that adequate, all we could justifiably ask for. Not only that, but he was lost in his memory and became, for him, loquacious. By loquacious I mean that Saunders would pole his skiff for a bit, his head turning mechanically, and then allow some words to fall quietly past his lips. And through this process, the following story got told.

Young Ansil Saunders was inspired by his meeting with Dr. King. He was likewise, I suppose, inspired by his friendship with Adam Clayton Powell, who had, upon his arrival in Washington, challenged the informal regulations forbidding black representatives from using Capitol facilities reserved for members only. Because what would happen, on the tiny isle of Bimini, is that at lunchtime the local fishing guides would drop their clients at the Big Game Club, and they themselves would remain outside, clustered at a little table and eating bagged lunches. Ansil saw this as patently unfair, and he began to exhort his colleagues to change it. When he first suggested that they enter the establishment, sit down and refuse to leave, they to a man begged off. Ansil was not easily dissuaded, though. He sat down at a table in the club and stared forward obdurately (obduracy, as we've seen, being one of the bright colours in his makeup) and did not respond when he was asked to leave. The management told staff to ignore the man, so Ansil went hungry that day, but he was back the next, sitting at the same table. Again he went without. The following day Saunders had company at the table, two of the other guides having decided to join him. And the next day there were more, and Ansil reported that soon all of the guides were sitting in the restaurant, where they were frantically ignored by the waitstaff. "It took about a month,"

Bonefish Saunders remembered, "but finally they took our order and brought us food."

Of course, it is more important that Bimini be integrated and harmonious than that I be mollycoddled and falsely flattered by a fishing guide, and I don't guess that any one man would be capable of the two actions. So while I still maintain that Bonefish Saunders lacked social graces in much the same way as fish lack tap-dancing skills, I ended the day with great admiration for the man. And yes, Jake and I did hear the hundred and fifty-second sam. Saunders drove his beautiful wooden boat back into the grove of mans, and at a certain point cut the motor. He looked around, checked his bearings and then stood on his poling platform. Bonefish Saunders placed one hand over his heart, and with the other he gesticulated at the twisted roots of life that surrounded us. "Oh, Lord," he began, "we see Thy wonders in all of Thy creation . . ."

This psalm was quite a bit longer than the preceding one hundred and fifty-one, and Ansil planted his lead right there in the first line, so I don't have to transcribe much more. It was a beautiful little pocket of time that we three sat in and, like Dr. King's, my eyes welled up with tears.

And if I ever have to write a Nobel Prize acceptance speech (hint, hint), I know just where I'm going to go.

THE FEMINIZATION OF FISHING

You should know that I am currently sitting in an inadequately heated basement apartment. I am working at my computer because sleep seems awfully far away. To put a stake through the heart of the thing, I have been thrown out of the matrimonial home. I hope you aren't made uncomfortable by this admission. I only bring it up to point out that if I have entitled something "The Feminization of Fishing," you can rest assured that the insight I intend to share was hard-earned.

Because I am not the most enlightened of fellows.

Let me take us all back a few weeks, when things were sunnier both figuratively and literally. I was in the Bahamas with my friend Jake, who is, perhaps, slightly more enlightened than I.

But not much more.

We had gone in pursuit of the elusive bonefish. This was, as the astute reader will realize, our second venture in this regard. A year before, on the island of Bimini and abiding the guiding hand of Bonefish Ansil, we'd managed to catch a brace of bone each. But that was with regular tackle, and we'd decided this time to try with fly gear.

Jake and I went to Elbow Cay on the island of Abaco, which is skinny and elongated and forms part of the spine of the Bahamian cluster. We engaged a guide named Maitland Lowe, although he preferred the monicker "Bonefish Dundee," because (a) he hunted bonefish and (b) he was blond, sunburnt and looked a little like Paul Hogan, the actor who portrayed Crocodile Dundee. Maitland was even more weather-beaten than Hogan, what we must perforce call "weather-beaten up." His skull was covered with strips of desiccated flesh toasted to a crisp brown. Maitland was a handsome enough fellow, possessing well-made and regular features: eyes, nose, mouth and cigarette. I include cigarette in that list because Bonefish Dundee was never without a smoke caught between his lips.

Jake and I showed up at the dock at eight o'clock in the morning. I will confess that I was saddled by a monstrous hangover; the monkey on my back had wrapped itself around my head and was blasting out streams of putrid effluvia. I had succumbed, the night before, to First Nighter's Syndrome, which afflicts many people upon arrival at a holiday destination. There are several factors at work: excitement, sleep deprivation and, in my case, alcoholism. At any rate, I had overimbibed to an unseemly extent. There were two beds in the cabin Jake and I shared, and although my buddy gave me first dibs, I had apparently grown dissatisfied with my choice in the middle of the night and crawled into bed with him. This is beginning to sound like an address made before the assembled at an AA meeting; I am only relating it to indicate that I was not at my best, not prepared to fight either the piscatorial, or the psychic, battles that awaited me that fine day.

BONEFISH Dundee behaved as any good fishing guide would, casting surly glances at the pair of us and rubbing at a fresh maculation on his nose. Jake roared, "Morning, Cap'n!" He actually did roar; Jake actually does. Maitland Lowe nodded, flicked the brim of his baseball cap, spat out his butt and relit, all in a trice. Then he accepted our cargo, which consisted of fly rods, tackle boxes and a couple of juice boxes. I was so dehydrated from my tussle with the bottle that these juice boxes represented survival. Which is to say, should I survive that day and get shipwrecked thereafter, the juice boxes might save my sorry life. As it was, my thirst was monstrous and furry, and the juice boxes were worse than useless.

Jake felt called upon to point out my condition to Bonefish Dundee. "He got pissed last night," announced Jake. Maitland's mouth slowly rippled into something resembling a smile. I mistook this for fraternal sympathy; there was much of the boozehound in Bonefish Dundee, although I was to find out he was now teetotal. His cryptic grin, in retrospect, was likely one of disdain. Perhaps our relationship got off on the wrong foot right then and there, but being me, I like to place blame on people other than myself. Like on my buddy Jake, who, as Maitland revved the engine, sat down on the bench beside and indicated a small space between himself and Bonefish Dundee. "Come on, Quarrington!" he roared. "Sit your fat ass down here!"

"Ha!" Maitland found this a highly amusing gibe. "Fat ass," he repeated, as though he'd never heard the expression before and believed Jake to be its originator. Then he ventured to see if he could use the phrase correctly himself. "Yeah, sit your fat ass down!" The completion of the phrase was coincident with his slamming the engine into forward gear, so I did indeed sit my fat ass down, emphatically so. Jake and Maitland erupted gleefully. Of course, Maitland couldn't erupt gleefully without immediately horking up a nicotine-stained lung.

As we motored out to the fishing grounds, Jake engaged Maitland in more of this banter. My name came up quite often. "You'll have seen better casters than me, you'll have seen worse," Jake judged. "Quarrington there is pitiful."

"Pitiful," said Maitland scornfully. "Quarrington."

Now, I am not so thin-skinned as to have taken real umbrage at any of this. In point of fact I was every bit as good a caster as Jake, especially with my own equipment, my fly rod being nicely balanced and personalized, a small swale carved out of the corked butt for my thumb to lie comfortably. Unfortunately my own equipment was useless to me that day, seeing as I'd trampled upon it sometime during the previous evening's sodden activities. Jake and I (I recalled dimly) had been practising our casting, so as not to embarrass ourselves in front of the guide. I'd laid my rod aside in order to do something (what was it, oh, yeah, get a drink) and I ignored the primary rule of rod maintenance, which is never to leave it lying around on the ground. As I returned from my errand, my gait heavy and erratic, I heard a small crunching sound and saw that I had neatly broken the thing in twain. "Er, shit," I said that night, although I will admit I do that sort of thing a lot, bust equipment (I do it stone-cold sober, too), so I didn't piss and moan too long. I mourned in a vague way the loss of a few hundred bucks and then I left to do something, what was it, oh, yeah, get a drink.

But the sad correlative truth didn't hit home until the next morning, that being: I was going to have to use Jake's gear. And Jake's gear, to my mind, was about as balanced as a cow on a clothesline. Jake could work the thing. Indeed, Jake could make line fly out, gracefully extruded through the guides. He'd even worked out his own idiosyncratic double-hauling technique, yanking line with his free hand and finding a moment to kick at the butt with his palm, adding power to the cast. My own efforts with Jake's equipment were less than satisfactory. Perhaps it was necessary to have this palm-kick trick in one's arsenal. Perhaps it was simply the fact that Jake's stuff was six inches longer than mine; anyway, you'll let me know when you figure I'm about done making excuses. What's that? Oh, fine. Back to the scene.

Maitland pushed the throttle into neutral, and his skiff bucked and shuddered and came to an abrupt halt. We had arrived at the fishing grounds, archipelagoed with stands of mangrove. Maitland looked around, picked up his pole (one end had been carved into a lethal-looking point, making Maitland's pole officially a *pike*) and climbed onto the platform. He began to propel us soundlessly through the shallows. "All right," Maitland said quietly, "one of you get on up there."

"You go first, Paul," suggested Jake, which had the ring of good manners but was really anything but. The "up there" that Maitland referred to was at the bow of the boat, where there was enough wood between the gunwales—a bulging triangle maybe three feet across at its widest—to allow a fly caster to stand tall, scan the waters and wield his stick. I climbed up, dumped a few yards of line at my feet, adjusted my sunglasses and waited.

"Bonefish, sir," muttered Maitland. "A pair of 'em. Three o'clock."

I turned to my right. The rubber on the soles of my shoes made a small squeak, I mean, *really* small, something along the lines of the sound a mouse might make when faking an orgasm.

"No, sir," said Maitland. "You've spooked 'em. They're gone."

After a few more minutes of silence: "Bonefish, sir. Eleven o'clock."

Swinging my upper body gently to the left, I peered at the water and saw, of course, nothing.

"Where?"

"There, sir. Forty feet away, sir."

"Oh, yeah! I see it!"

"There's six of them, sir."

I started casting, letting out line, concentrating on making a nice tight loop to cut through what had become a stiff breeze—

"Too much false casting, sir. They've gone."

Let's see, what else could go wrong? Bear in mind that I have yet to actually lay a cast down upon the water.

"Bonefish, sir. Two o'clock. Fifty feet away. He's lying aslant the boat, sir. Keep looking. You'll see him."

"Hey! I see him!"

"Very good, sir."

"Let me just cast to him, *uh!*"

"No, sir."

"No."

"The fish is gone, sir. He was spooked by your lay-down. Even though it happened quite some distance away from him, sir."

"Jake, you give it a try."

"Yes," said Maitland with undisguised enthusiasm. "Let's have Jake up there. Quarrington . . . sit your fat ass down."

THE chiding continued unabated. It actually got a lot worse, because over the next few hours Maitland and Jake established a fast friendship, bound together, chiefly, by their abusive disdain of the pitiful creature named Quarrington. Maitland tended to give me one chance up on the bow, one crack at fucking up, before suggesting that Jake remount. And I was pretty good at fucking up. Like any skill, casting is adversely affected by self-consciousness. Plus, I was using Jake's equipment . . . but you'll let me know when I'm done making excuses. Yes, okay, fine.

"Bonefish, sir. It's right in fucking front of you, sir. No, sir, it's gone. The fish won't wait around forever while you stand there. With your fat ass. Jake, get on up there."

Not that Jake didn't fuck up. He actually threw his line back upon Maitland, and the fly carved a little gash in the guide's sunburnt cheek. Bonefish Dundee roared with laughter, and affectionately suggested that Jake practise more. It was as though this gash was the blood ceremony needed to really cement their relationship. "Bonefish, Jake."

"Aye-aye, Skipper."

"Aye-aye," Maitland repeated, marvelling at Jake's endless verbal invention.

"Bonefish, Jakey!"

Jakey? I reflected that Maitland never used my Christian name. He occasionally called me "Quarrington," but only if he had some comment to make about my fat ass. That's when I realized that the unctuous "sir" Maitland employed actually stood in for something other. From that point forward I couldn't help but hear this whenever Maitland spoke to me.

"Bonefish, asshole. Forty feet away, asshole. Right over there, asshole. No, asshole. He's gone. Asshole."

WE should discuss the guide/client relationship at this point, which has ever been a little complicated. (Don't worry. I intend to make good on the title of the piece, "The Feminization of Fishing," but it's necessary to establish the traditional male parameters.) Guiding may seem a simple enough business: the client gives the guide money; the guide supplies expertise, specialized equipment and, usually, lunch. "Specialized equipment" refers to stuff that the angler would not necessarily own and which is specific to the quarry or the area being fished. Therefore, Maitland took one look at the flies Jake and I had (flies that had cost us a pretty penny in Toronto) and blew a derisive raspberry. He produced some gaudy monstrosities that looked as if they had been tied by—and though I search my imagination for phrases relating to blindness and cretinism, I can do no better than to suggest that these flies looked as if they had been tied by *me*. Other guides might supply more tackle. For example, if one is going salmon fishing, the rods are already sprouting out of their holders in the captain's boat. As I say, the client can also reasonably expect lunch, and drinks, although there is an understanding that the client himself should bring along some drinks, and snacks, so as not to *assume* the provision of victuals, because said assumption would reinforce the uncomfortable master/slave template that is always there in the shadows. No one really likes to be involved in a master/slave relationship (not unless it involves leather, stiletto heels and, er, perhaps I am ranging outside the purview of this story). As a client, I am very conscientious about treating the guide with respect. I am paying for his knowledge, not his subservience. Guides tend to resist the master/slave thing by being, well, *uppity*.

Take Bonefish Ansil. The year previous, when Jake and I were fishing for bone on traditional tackle, Ansil had instructed me to slip into the water and stalk about the flats in search of fish. I did so; that is, I eased my body over the side of the boat and began to wade very gingerly—

"You walk like a goddamn *elephant!*" shouted Bonefish Ansil.

Well, maybe. Maybe I am clumsy and oafish and steatopygous. But I'll thank you not to mention that if I'm ponying up two hundred bucks an hour.

There is another factor at work here. Guides have careers to maintain, and an endless succession of hapless bumbling losers would do those careers great damage. If, day after day, his clients returned fishless, a guide's reputation would diminish and his trade would suffer. Many guides therefore exhibit annoyance, and often anger, if the client can't cut the mustard. One is sometimes berated for poor technique and/or lapses in judgement/execution. Jake has a stoic attitude toward this; he feels that too much of our adulthood is spent in complacency, that it does a man good to have someone say *what you're doing is just not good enough.* He may have a point. The guides are usually nicer to Jake than they are to me, maybe because he's a better angler, maybe because he sets this tone of Quarrington-chiding—

AT least that's what I accused him of after that first day of fishing with Bonefish Dundee.

"What do you mean?" Jake asked innocently.

"Well, I mean, you began the day by insulting me and made it seem like grand sport. *Sit your fat ass down,* indeed. And you told him things about me. Told him I was hung over, that I was a bad caster—"

"I didn't tell him that you crawled into bed with me last night. I might have made some hay with that, don't you think, if I was really doing what you're accusing me of?"

"All I'm saying is, try to be a bit nicer to me tomorrow."

I will admit that Jake did try to be a bit nicer to me the following day, but Maitland was having none of it. Maitland's new hobby was being insulting to Quarrington, which he seemed to understand was an activity very popular and widely accepted in Canada. Maitland felt himself fortunate to be the first native Bahamian to become aware of the pastime, and he engaged fully at every opportunity.

"There's a nice place for your fat ass," he said, glowering at me and winking at Jake.

I was not hung over that day or, to be more precise, my hangover was manageable and not crippling, so I delivered my casts with much more accuracy and aplomb. This mattered to the fish not a whit. They would see the fly land and glance at one another. "Who threw that, Jake or Quarrington?" If the answer were the latter, they would disappear. Jake's offerings they would survey, though, maybe even approach, and round about noon of that next day, one of them bit.

I was standing about a hundred feet away from the boat at the time, because Maitland had instructed me to wade about, I believe as punishment for some angling shortcoming on my part. I was alerted by an exuberant "Attago, Jakey!" and saw my friend holding on to his fly rod with knuckle-blanching intensity.

As we have seen, the bonefish's first strategy, when hooked, is to fly off toward the end of the world. There's not much the angler can do to dissuade it. Eventually the fish may rethink its plan, and sometimes it has drawn sufficient line from the reel that the accumulated drag slows the fish down. Bonefish Ansil, you may recall from his shirt, had been the guide for the world-record bonefish, which weighed in at a remarkable sixteen pounds. When he recounted the tale to Jake and me, he said that the fish stripped line off the reel until there was but a foot or two left on the spool. "For the life of me," he told us, "I don't know what made that fish decide to stop. But it did."

And Jake's fish stopped, too. Soon the fly reel was sputtering intermittently, and then there was a second or two of dead calm.

"All right, Jakey," said Maitland. "She's coming back."

Since phase two of bonefish-escape strategy is to fly straight back at the angler, it becomes necessary to take up line at a commensurate rate; too much slack will allow the fish many opportunities for freedom. So Jake began to reel as fast as he could, with Maitland exhorting him to do so even faster. "Reel, sir!" Maitland shouted, which made me feel a little better, because I knew Maitland was really saying, "Reel, asshole!" Jake reeled faster than was physically possible, or that's the impression I got from the lines carved into his face, the sweat popping out of his brow. He fumbled at one point as his hand spasmed into gnarly tree roots, slipping away from the handle. The fish flew out of the water then, full of spiteful glee, as if to proclaim, "I'm free, I'm free!" But perhaps Jake had been reeling fast enough to actually *reverse* time (a concept you might understand if you've read enough Superman comic books). He reset his hand on the reel and pulled back, and he was still tight to the fish.

Then began the battle at close quarters, the fish relying on a repertoire of feints, sorties and rollovers. "Keep your rod tip up, Jakey," said Maitland. It's not as if Jake didn't *know* that, but it was more a theoretical concept, given the seven pounds of silver muscle insisting that the rod tip point *down*. Man and fish struggled for many long moments and eventually the fish grew weary. I don't believe the fish grew as weary as my friend Jake did, but—and I make no apologies, this is assuredly the angler's ace in the hole—Jake didn't have a hook in his lip. So the fish grew weary and had no place to turn. Maitland leapt into the water, trailed behind the bonefish as it made its last desperate zigs and zags. Then Bonefish Dundee reached downward into the water and raised the catch toward the sun. It caught the light and was blinding.

AFTER that triumph, the two buddies, Jake and Maitland, decided they'd try their hand at something new. Jake had long wanted to catch a barracuda on his fly rod, so Maitland roared off for a little bay that he knew held the creatures in numbers.

In the section above, wherein I ruminated briefly on the client-guide relationship, I didn't mention another cause for resentment that crops up from time to time, especially with younger guides: they resent the fact that the client is fishing and they're not. There was an element of this in Maitland Lowe; he was a very vigorous man, and he bristled with energy that he was eager to spend. Because barracuda fishing was not technically the kind of fishing he'd been engaged to oversee, Maitland decided now to become a participant. He stood backward in his boat, one hand on the throttle, the other wielding a fly rod. As he piloted the boat around the bay (at quite a pace, too, the engine howling, and yes, your mental picture of the scene is quite accurate: he couldn't see where he was going), Maitland leisurely drove a long cast near the shoreline. Man, it was quite a poke. Bonefish Dundee is invariably Abaco's champion in the bonefish derby, and he is sent to represent his island in the Bahamian tournaments. I understood then something of his annoyance and frustration with me and, I suspect, most of his clientele. (I was reminded of Bobby Orr's brief coaching career, which came to naught despite all of the legendary hockey player's skill and experience. Because Orr would say to a defenceman, "All you have to do is take the puck from behind your own blueline, skate around everyone in the centre and feed a perfect pass to the left winger." And the hapless player would reply, "Huh?")

Maitland caught a barracuda, displayed it, asked if we would like to eat it for dinner that night. We declined, because we'd heard there was a disease sometimes in the fish, *ciguera,* so that eating one could prove fatal.

"No, don't worry about that. That never happens," said Maitland, although he paused a moment for reflection and added, "Mind you, that's how my father died, eating a bad 'cuda."

My turn came, and I cast and flipped out line, and we yip-yip-yipped around the bay a few times before Maitland gestured irritably, told me to reel up. "Quarrington," he snorted disdainfully, "can't even catch a 'cuda."

That became the refrain for the rest of the day. Bonefish Dundee finally understood why Quarrington-insulting was

Canada's national sport. A lot of people can't catch a bonefish—
only Quarrington can't catch a 'cuda.

"CAN'T catch a 'cuda."

I heard these words, I swear to God I did, as I entered the
imbibing establishment that evening. I swung around and saw
Maitland standing at the bar, his wrinkled elbows folded upon it,
but he gave no indication of having seen me. Jake and I continued
along until we found a couple of free stools. The little barroom,
affixed to the resort we were staying at, was more crowded than it
usually was, so we were distanced from Bonefish Dundee and there
were plenty of people in between, mostly honeymooning couples
in bathing suits. (That was another factor playing upon my mood;
the place we were staying was popular with newlyweds, scantily
clad and moony with passion. We were there the evening of
February 14, which meant that Jake and I had a very romantic dinner, just the two of us, the patio table adorned with rose petals and
bathed in moonlight.) We ordered drinks, and Jake began to prat-
tle away, telling me some story designed to alter my state of mind.
I was melancholic and overcast; the story failed to cheer me, not
only because I'd heard it before (I think I've heard all of Jake's stories before), but because I was simply not to be cheered. Instead, I
rehearsed the story I would tell upon my return to Toronto, how
my guide was nasty and insulting, how Bonefish Dundee had

chided me relentlessly and made me lose all confidence in my angling abilities, indeed, how he took away any claim I might ever have *had* to angling abilities, seeing as I had achieved this nadir of ineptitude, the inability to catch a 'cuda.

At the beginning of this process I imagined myself telling the tale to fellow fishermen. I made much of Maitland's sun-withered appearance and water-weird ways. (I have forgotten to mention that one afternoon, while wading, Maitland spotted a little shark and wrestled briefly with the creature, his intention being to throw the mini-jaws into the boat so that it might surprise and amuse his good buddy Jake.) I suppose I was hoping to make Bonefish Dundee sound like some sort of a natural, a Caliban, *half a fish and half a monster.* Then I began to prepare the story for the women in my life, my wife, my neighbour Jill. I began to tell them how this Maitland Lowe was mean and nasty and insulting—

"Did you talk to him?"

"Huh?"

Jake, in the middle of his story, repeated his last sentence, thinking I'd directed the *huh* at him. But I'd really spoken it aloud to these women in my mind, both of whom had asked, "Did you talk to this Bonefish Dundee?"

"Well, no, I didn't talk to him—"

"Why not?"

Why not? Because men don't really talk about things like that. It seems more, well, I guess *effective* isn't quite the word, it seems more *natural* to simply brood and drink too much and remain miserable . . .

And thus was I shoved a baby step closer to enlightenment.

"I'm going to go talk to him," I announced, leaping off my barstool.

"Talk to who?"

"Bonefish fucking Dun . . . Maitland. I'm going to go talk to Maitland."

I made my way through the crowd, quashing crests of misgiving that peaked into nausea, and shouldered in beside my guide.

"Maitland," I began.

"Hello." Maitland tapped his finger on the bar, demanding another Coca-Cola. He took a moment to smoke a couple of cigarettes and then returned his attention to me.

"It seems to me," I began, "that we got off on the wrong foot."

"Aye." He really said that, *aye*. I made a connection then. Maitland, being a white Bahamian, was likely the descendant of pirates. Fine time to make *that* connection, I chastised myself. But there was no turning back. I was driven on by the voices of women demanding with ageless wisdom, "Did you talk to him?"

So I talked to him. I told him how I *felt*, dammit. I said I understood that it might have started off as the sort of good-natured insulting banter in which men indulge, but it had gone *way* beyond that. "Not only am I not catching any fish—and I admit

I'm a poor fisherman, but I swear to God I'm not half as bad as I seem to be when I'm with you—anyway, not only am I not catching any fish, but I am not enjoying myself."

Bonefish Dundee considered what I'd said. And then, alarmingly, his face fell. It swayed and collapsed like a suspension bridge in a Category 5 hurricane. Maitland Lowe looked at me miserably and said, "I'm sorry."

ALL right, let's make a quick cut to the following day, when Jake and I are once again fishing with Maitland Lowe, the legendary Bonefish Dundee (for *free*, as things turn out), and we find this kind of thing happening.

"Nice cast, sir!"

"Now, Maitland, I know it wasn't a good cast."

"Very nearly was, sir."

And although I failed to catch a bonefish on fly tackle that day, I don't believe that even a frolicking ten-pounder would have been as satisfying as hearing the words, "Bonefish. Eleven o'clock. Paul."

Which brings me back to my current situation: living in a friend's basement, booted out of the family home, etc. It is not at all a good situation, and I am not likely to change it by sitting here brooding and drinking too much and feeling miserable.

Luckily I learned a valuable lesson about communication from bonefishing with Bonefish Dundee. I have learned that if one has a problem with another human being, one should address it. Mind-boggling stuff, really, to your average angler.

But enlightenment—like a fish—is where you find it.

FISHING THROUGH DISASTER

I N the early evening of September 11, 2001, I strung up my fly
rod, pulled on my chest waders, walked across the street and
went trout fishing. This was in Calgary, Alberta, which is either a
small city or a huge town, by which I mean that it has been able to
metropilate without damaging its cordial relationship with Nature.
Although I had to dodge traffic whilst traversing Memorial Drive,
once I descended the scarp on the other side, I had a reasonable
chance of taking a fish in the Bow. There was a little island there,
in the middle of the river, and my routine was to position myself
across from its head and make my way downriver, fishing the fast
water between the bank and its rubbly shore. Across from me, pelicans stared, silently communicating the notion *no fish here*, but I
knew they were just trying to chase away the competition.

I threw out a modest length of line. My fly was small and
headed with a golden bead, which drew the leader down toward the
bottom. I mended a couple of times, watched the Bow drag fly line,
caught my breath and tensed when the maximum length was

achieved and the fly would—obeying the laws of physics—gently ascend from the bottom. This is when fish were likely to be caught.

Usually as I fished the Bow across from my apartment, passersby would slow on the walkway above, watch for a minute or two, inquire as to my luck and offer encouragement. That didn't happen that particular evening; for one thing, there were precious few people passing by, and those who did eyed me darkly and hurried along.

It was an odd thing I was doing, fishing on that evening, because that morning, as you well know, disaster of an unexampled order had taken place. Many people had died and our image of this planet had been altered profoundly. As I fished, hours after the tragedy, confusion and fear were King Stork, and the sensible (at any rate, the meekly human) thing to do was to gather with loved ones in front of a television screen and pray in various ways.

But I had elected to fish. For one thing, I had no loved ones, at least none that were anywhere proximate. My family was back in Toronto, although I am using the word *family* in a fairly technical manner, because mine had disintegrated. My wife and I had separated; finances and friction had forced this move to Calgary. I spoke to my children on the telephone, of course, and knew that they still loved me, *anyway,* the point is there was no one to gather with, so I didn't. I fished. Most evenings when I fished, there were other anglers within my sight, a couple both upriver and down, but on the evening of September 11 I fished all alone.

Not that I wasn't in a stupifyingly grim mood. I'd had a lousy year—besides the marital collapse, my father had died suddenly the previous spring, and to top it off there was this thing, you know, the end of the world as we know it—and fishing was not so much an elective activity as the only one I was capable of. The type of angling I was doing, drifting a nymph, is repetitive to the point of ritual. I worked the water close by, pulled out more line and shot for the middle, pulled out more line still and tried to work the seams that curled around the little naked island in the middle of the river. Then I'd take three or four steps downriver and do it all again. It suited my spiritual numbness.

Isaak Walton decreed that fishing was a contemplative pursuit. (For this reason, it was allowed to the clergy, although they were forbidden to hunt, which is why I do the one thing without doing the other.) So I contemplated things, although the very word has connotations of order and logic, and really what I was doing was floating in thoughts like a shipwrecked man might float in a sea full of debris and sharks.

The first thought that occurred, and the most facile, was that the fish had no idea anything terrible had happened, and went about their business with efficient custom. Human beings were trying to go about their business, I suppose, but did so with a certain lead-footedness. I was working on a television series in Calgary, and a colleague and I had spent some hours that day "breaking story," as they say in that biz, although every ten minutes or so we would bolt from the table and go to stare out the window, as if to make sure that the planet was still there. And we would return to our seats, shaking our heads and lowering our eyes, because there seemed to be something quite shameful about working on a light-hearted comedy/drama. The fish, in their ignorance, continued to act as they ever did; at one point a fish took a run at my fly, causing a momentary tightening of the line. Then it was gone.

Mind you, I am only assuming that no great piscine disaster had taken place. It could be that some dastard had lobbed a stick of dynamite into the Bow upriver, causing many silver corpses to ascend to the surface, the vault of their world. In which case, the fish were behaving normally despite this. Perhaps the most normal reaction to the observance of disaster (at least the most normal as dictated by Mother Nature, that powerful but grim lady) is "Whew, I'm glad that wasn't me." Human beings don't allow themselves that reflection, but I'll bet fish do (or so proceeded my contemplation). I'll bet fish allow themselves that reflection, but only for a second or two, because they know the correlative: another disaster exists just up- or downriver, one that may claim them.

Of course, it occurred to me then that a fish leads a pretty damned prescribed existence and isn't really allowed the luxury of abandoning its business. At that moment I was envious of this fact. Look, I told myself, at how complicated your life has become. I ran through some, by no means all, of the events that had led to my arrival in Calgary. I recalled betrayal and heartache (and let me make it clear, this was the awful stuff that I had meted out, not received). I longed then for the fish's clarity of purpose, that's it, *clarity of purpose*, and I suppose I was approximating that with my angling. I stepped sideways in the river, stumbling over slick rocks, the water high and pressing in upon my chest, making me feel as though I wanted to cry. (I'm pretty sure it was water pressure that made me feel as though I wanted to cry.) And I repeated the process, trying to do it with skill, which somehow pushed the activity closer to Magick. I worked the water close by, I worked the middle, finally I drew in my breath, mustered my resolve and threw for the seams that enveloped the island. I believe even the pelicans were impressed.

I contemplated the cycle. When standing in a river, it's impossible for a human being *not* to contemplate the cycle, the Great Wheel of Life, just as a human being must contemplate his or her own insignificance when standing underneath a panoply of stars. There's some comfort in knowing that we all are part of a greater thing, that we swim for a while in the river and then leave it to others to complete the journey to the source. And do you know what kind of comfort it is? Cold, of course, frigid. I envied the fish their ability to accept it. (Another human assumption, because I have no way of registering fishy complaint. But I somehow imagine that when a trout spies a fly, just before racing off he turns back to his mates and says, "If anything goes wrong, fellas, I just want you to know, it's been a slice.") So I tried to approximate this thinking in dealing with my father's death. I told myself, "Well, the Old Man had to die sooner or later," just as fish might say, "Did you see what happened to Rudy? He fell for the gaudiest streamer fly *ever*." But I couldn't do it convincingly, because I don't believe human beings accept the cycle any more than we accept our own insignificance. We have our *selves*, you know, we have our identities and our loves and our hobbies and our secrets, and I keep repeating the *our* because we mean these things to be *ours;* we are not willing to let them be spun by the Great Wheel of Life. We are willing to contemplate our own insignificance only because we know we can leave the heavenly firmament behind. We can say, "Let's go back inside now. I'll make you some osso bucco. I have a secret recipe."

I next applied my contemplation to time, because time and insignificance go hand in hand. Also, it had been some time now, and I had yet to catch a fish. The Bow, as it ploughs through downtown Calgary, yields its bounty only sparingly. I had stepped out of it fishless many times, occasions marked not so much by failure as by lack of success, a distinction that comes naturally to the compulsive angler. And if it seems to you that my contemplation has gotten completely derailed here, let me assure you that it does all connect. We'll begin at this insignificance thing, the weak, unnurturing succour we give ourselves when cold-cocked by misfortune. Not only are our lives small, they are also fleeting, as flitting and frenzied as a mosquito's. I realized, standing in the Bow, that *that* is, in fact, why we fish. Although this is not because we *may as well*, this is no semi-sedate version of "We're here for a good time, not for a long time."

Let us imagine that our lives were longer. Let us imagine that our lives were 5,000 years long, long enough to grant them a smidgin of significance. In many ways it sounds appealing, because there would be lots more time to do the things we enjoy. There would be more sex and more good food and more fun, or so one might imagine. But what would be lost is the idea of fortune, the illusion that the gods are grinning down upon us. Angling would lose all of its appeal—except with regard to the fish taken for the supper table, I suppose—because in the hours, days, months devoted to it, all manner of fish would be taken, from teeny little tiddlers to battleship-size bruisers. Do you see what I'm getting at? There would be no surprise, only soul-deadening eventuality. So my theory is that because we can only offer minutes here and there to the pursuit, when we catch a trophy (I speak metaphorically, being against the concept of hanging dead things on walls), we have accomplished something that should only occur in a longer life, the 5,000-year variety. We have therefore lent our much shorter life significance.

I seem to have drifted a very long way from the source of my contemplation, the disaster that befell thousands on the morning of September 11. But having arrived at this place, it was much easier to mourn the lives lost. Because I realized that, while only a small percentage may have been anglers, they likely all had some sort of pursuit that accomplished the same thing. Some may have been habitues of bingo parlours, some may have purchased lottery tickets. What I'm saying is they all did something, and did this something under heaven and invited grace and luck to anoint them. And although they may have been destroyed by misfortune, I prayed that they had all had moments of serendipity.

And I had a moment there, in the Bow River. Not that I took a big fish, but I took a fish, a twelve-inch rainbow trout. I would describe to you the capture, except it was uneventful and by no means the point of my angling that evening. What was important to me was that moment of good fortune, during which I thought I could detect God trying to smile again.

THE IDEA OF ORDER
AT TSUNAMI LODGE

THIS is a piece that never got written.

I told some people that it would get written, but I never wrote it. I know it seems as if I'm writing it now, but I'm not, really. I'm writing about how and why it never got written.

I told the manager of Tsunami Lodge, near Campbell River on Vancouver Island, that the piece was going to be written. Not only that, I told this man it was going to be published. I was professionally vague as to where that might take place. "I have a relationship with a number of suitable organs," I said, chewing on my pen nib. I was chewing on my pen nib to illustrate to this man, the manager, that I was both pensive and a writer. A pensive writer, in point of fact. This was about the fifth pen I had ingested during our conversation.

"I see," he said doubtfully. *"Outdoor Life? Men's Journal?"*

I nodded, assuring the manager in my own little way that he had correctly named a couple of magazines.

My friend Jake stepped in. "I'm writing an article for *Prairie Business Magazine.*"

"Uh-huh."

"He really is," I rushed in, and then, seeing that I was doing damage, further eroding the manager's trust, I did what many writers do. I behaved like a pompous windbag. "I have a good title," I announced, although I didn't, or hadn't only moments before. "I'm going to call my article 'The Idea of Order at Tsunami Lodge.' "

"What does *that* mean?"

"After Stevens, of course, Wallace Stevens."

"*Prairie Business Magazine* has a pretty big circulation," put in Jake reassuringly.

I pressed on. "You see, in many ways this lodge has been *imposed* upon the landscape. It combats the chaos of the natural world with manifestations of civilization, put here by human will alone."

"Hmm. Interesting." The manager hadn't said that *hmm, interesting,* I'd said it, after a few fat moments of dumbfounded silence.

What the manager said was, rising from behind his desk, "Well, you know . . . make yourselves at home."

And then he was gone, and Jake took off his baseball cap and beat me about the ears for many moments.

Because it was Jake who had brokered the deal, and me who seemed likely to scupper it. The deal was this: Jake and I were staying, all expenses paid, at Tsunami Lodge. And—get this—Tsunami Lodge was the most expensive fishing resort on Vancouver Island, which is home to a great many very expensive fishing resorts. Tsunami Lodge cost the client a nice, round G-note a day. "But at least," the manager had explained, "we're not nickel-and-diming them. You know, some places, it's *this* for the room, and *this* for the meals, and *this* for the bar, and *this* for the guide, and *this* for the fishing licence . . . Here, it's just the one payment. Everything is looked after."

"Let me understand you," I said very journalistically. "There's an open bar?"

"There are several open bars. Why, there's one practically everywhere you look."

"Hmmm. Interesting."

So the deal was, Jake and I would come as guests for three full days and four nights (we'd arrived at five o'clock in the afternoon) and would pay the owners *no money*, and in return we would write articles about Tsunami Lodge. So, given that we could probably each get two or three thou for the articles, and were being cuffed three or four thou, this was like a six-thou deal going down here. Plus, we got to go fishing! I was confident that I could find some magazine eager to publish an article detailing my experiences and ruminations, even though all of the editors I had spoken with so far had not been interested.

"But it's not like any of our readers could actually afford to *go* there," one said.

(This is by way of being a flashback. This is the article that never got written, so issues of clumsiness don't concern us.)

"Your readers can't afford to go *any* of the places you print articles about."

"Sure, they can."

"No, they can't. If they could, they would be at those places fishing, and not sitting home reading your magazine."

"Paul . . ."

"Fishing magazines are for the angling-deprived. When are you people going to realize that? They are instruments of envy and heartbreak. So why can't I write about this Tsunami Lodge, or whatever the hell it's called, and they will read the article and weep forlornly."

"It is not our editorial mandate that our readership should weep forlornly."

"Why not? That's exactly what they're doing."

Anyway, Jake had made a sale, to this *Prairie Business Magazine*, because in that oil-clogged region of our planet there probably *are* people who can pony up a grand a day, but I had failed to raise even a congenial "Write it, we'll read it, we'll see." That hadn't prevented me from going on the trip, of course. My plan, so quixotic that even I never gave it voice or credence, was to write an article for *Gray's Sporting Journal*. Do you know that one? Excellent, excellent. Full of exquisitely written pieces about fishing far off and fine. (I am making an allusion to Isaak Walton there or, more pedantically, to Charles Cotton, Walton's often overlooked co-writer. That was the advice given to fly casters, to fish *far off and fine*, and good advice it is, too.) I knew that the editors of Gray's would likely place anything I sent them immediately into the waste bin, but there was a chance that if I came up with just the right literary angle, say, "The Idea of Order at Tsunami Lodge . . ."

JAKE and I investigated Tsunami Lodge. Sure enough, there were open bars almost everywhere we looked. I walked up to one and spied, in the great multitude of liquor bottles, some fine single malts lined up shoulder to shoulder. I indicated that I wanted, um, *that* one, and the bartender took a tumbler and inverted the designated bottle over it. Scotch began to fill the glass, and I realized with joy (tinged with apprehension) that the bartender was going to allow Scotch to gush until I told him to stop. "That's enough," I said quietly, and he handed me my tumbler. While Jake asked the bartender a few questions (dull ones, I figured, designed to satisfy the low-grade curiosity of businessmen on the Prairies), I wandered over to a little table where there was a box of fine cigars. I lit one, pocketed another, sat down in an easy chair and began to ruminate. Although it was early in the proceedings, I wanted to shape the article in my head. I wanted to somehow coalesce my vaporous thoughts into a more manageable cloud. But then the fishing boats began arriving back, and the guides discharged their clients, and before I knew it, it was time for dinner.

I'm going to skip over that meal (because, for reasons that shall become clear, the next night's repast was more noteworthy), and I'll skip over the evening (which involved a thorough journalistic investigation of *all* the open bars), and I will jump now, in this piece that never got written, to the next morning.

Jake and I arrived right on ungodly time, 6:00 A.M. or something, and the Dockmaster, who was an extraordinarily fetching woman (despite her yellow slickers), directed us to a specific boat. A man stood beside it, smoking a cigarette with a certain urgency, as if it were the last one he had and he was scheduled for execution, anyway. He had about four days' growth of beard on his face; he had eyes that looked as though some kid had used them to play marbles. We offered pleasantries, although, employing a tennis analogy, this fellow merely stood there and let our volleys go by, half turning to watch the balls bounce away.

We jumped into his boat and powered off.

I've examined, in a piece that *did* get written, the complex guide/client relationship, and I've furthermore expostulated on the complications arising from an angling threesome, guide/client/client, which become even more gnarly when one of those /clients is Jake. Jake likes to bond with the guide early on. I knew that Jake had his work cut out for him this time, because here's how those first interlocutions went:

"So, what's your name?"

The guide looked around for some long moments, giving it serious thought, not the answer so much as the process, the very act, of answering. You might have witnessed the same kind of thing in a police interrogation room. You might have seen someone with blood-spattered hands react identically to the question, "Where's the body?"

"Keith," he answered finally.

"Where are you from, Keith?" asked Jake.

Again there was a long delay before Keith replied, "Here and there."

Aha, thought I. *Jake's in trouble.*

Not only that, but later that morning Jake actually *got* into trouble. We had gone to a certain area where Mother Nature had contrived to build a kind of bowl, an arena, using the stands of Douglas fir to describe a large semicircle. There was a bite on, to use the argot of the West Coast salmon fisherman, so the place was crowded with boats, all motoring around, lengths of line dragging behind them. We were fishing with level-wind reels, which are sort of a cross between fly- and bait-casting tackle. That is to say, it is much easier to get line out than with a fly-fishing reel, but the experience of reclaiming line (especially when there is a fish on the other end) is thrillingly similar.

And I was hot, I was smoking. Translated into layperson's terms, I was pumped with grace and good fortune, so much so that I believed this example of randomness (the fish electing my bait and not Jake's) meant that I was highly skilled and able. This self-deception was so powerful that I actually played the coho nicely, bringing them to boat with a determination equal to the fishes' desire for escape. In doing so, I had earned some small words of admiration from the surly Keith. "Good," he said. (I guess that's only one small word of admiration, isn't it?) At one point I was playing a fish, watching the beast explode on the surface many yards behind the boat, and Keith was standing beside me, gaff in hand. Jake noticed that our boat was on a potential collision course with another. Jake knows boats, so he went to the stern and put his hands on the tiller.

"Get your hands off!" snapped Keith. He leapt backward, taking his position and righting the situation, and Jake sat down and sulked.

As giddy as I was with my angling success, in many ways it was diminishing my already tiny hopes of getting an article published in *Gray's Sporting Journal.* There was something a little off-putting about the number of boats in the bowl with the bite on, something plebian and ignoble. I had thought that I might make much of the majesty of the surroundings, the huge trees and convoluted water-ways, the way at high tide the black surface rippled and ripped with ferocity. But we debased that, in many ways, with our mindless putt-puttering, the two-way radio transmissions that crackled between the guides. "We had seven on, we put five in the boat." "We got three in the boat." It was big fun, but so are a great many unsavoury activities.

Keith would dispatch the fish with a wooden club that was

always near at hand. I kept a couple of fish, Jake kept a couple of fish, and we tried to decline as we caught more, but Keith would always think of a reason for dispatching. "I need a fish for dinner," he'd say, ka-whacking the thing on the head. Or, "This one's for the lodge." Ka-whack. I can only imagine that there was fierce competitiveness between the guides; anyway, more fish were dispatched than need have been. Again, something *Gray's Sporting Journal* doesn't really endorse. I wondered idly if there were some magazine called *Gray's Not Exactly Sporting Journal.*

The action was not constant, of course. Just as a professional football game has only about twelve minutes of actual action, though it may last four hours, a fruitful day of angling still contains large pockets of idle time. So we spent them telling jokes. Now, Jake knows some decent jokes. Keith, warming up a bit, offered a couple himself. His best one was about a bear, and it was pretty lame, coarse and homophobic. I myself know some great jokes. I'll give them some titles for easy reference: the Chee-chee joke, the Cindy Crawford, the Charlie, the Robinson Crusoe. You may wonder why I'm telling you this, but since this piece never got written there is no reason to exclude things. And this, this joke business, is significant to me. It is kind of a personal thing. It has mostly to do with my relationship with Jake, and perhaps might be best taken up between the two of us. But too late for that, because here I go . . .

We put into dock late in the afternoon, fully eleven hours after we left. (This might have been craftiness on the part of management: *We've got to keep that journalist away from the open bars, or he'll cost us a fortune. Keep him out fishing all day!*) We gave our catch over to the comely Dockmaster, who held a clipboard and recorded our wishes for its preparation. For example, I said that I wanted some of it rendered into steaks, some of it smoked, some of it canned, and three or four weeks later I received a lovely shipment in the mail that fed my family and myself for weeks. I calculate that the meat only cost about $700 a pound, or would have if not for the deal, the deal that I now knew I could never keep my end of up. (If only because of a propensity to write sentences like that one, syntactically troubled to say the least.)

We showered, hit a couple of the open bars and then went for dinner.

Dinner was held, medieval-style, in a large room with broad wooden tables laid out along all four walls. I half expected troubadours, buffoons and fire-eaters to come wheeling into the empty square, but they never materialized, just an endless series of young Native women wearing an odd black uniform and carrying great silver salvers loaded with foodstuffs. They seemed to have cuisine from every quarter of the world, with all the major food groups (and many of the minor ones) represented. One gentleman stared at the offerings and announced, "You know what? I'm just a meat-and-potatoes guy. What I'd like is a steak about *yea thick*, bloody, and a baker." This was brought to him almost immediately.

Many of the people attending the feast were accustomed to this kind of prerogative. One gentleman we recognized as the owner of a Canadian hockey franchise. Others were more anonymous, but we could tell they were bigwigs and muck-a-mucks. There were women and children there, very attractive, exuding the kind of wholesomeness that only great wads of money can buy. One entire flank was taken up by Mexicans, nine or ten of them, who lit into the food with unreserved gluttony and swilled it down with beer, tequila and Scotch. The story on these men, which we'd picked up from a loquacious barman, was that they owned the bottling contract for Coca-Cola in their homeland, and were therefore worth quadrillions of pesos.

Oh, I should mention that there were also a couple of men there of evidently more modest means. We'd met them upon our arrival, Ted and Todd. They worked in sales for a big pharmaceutical company in Kamloops, British Columbia, and their reward for eclipsing their colleagues was this sojourn at Tsunami Lodge. They were tired, pale and sullen; we'd learned, during a brief exchange over open-bar drinks, that they'd gone fishless that day.

So that was the crowd, and I was rather intimidated, but my friend Jake is a clubbable man, and at the first available opportunity announced, "You know what we did today? We told *jokes.*"

The assembled pressed Jake to tell one. He required little pressing. He launched into the Chee-chee classic.

One of my jokes.

It made for much merriment, so Jake was importuned to tell another.

Cindy Crawford. *Mine.*

Great mirth.

I turned and stared at my former friend.

"Hey, Paul," he said, "*you* tell one."

"Okay." I reviewed my repertoire, what was left of it, but before I could decide, Jake offered a suggestion. "Tell the one about the bear."

"What?"

"You know, the hunter and the bear."

It dawned that he was encouraging me to relate that lame joke of Keith's. "I know a better one," I said with urgency, but the gathered were with Jake on this one.

"The bear!" they demanded. "Tell us the one about the bear!"

I did so. There were no huzzahs of glee. Many didn't get it. Mothers clucked their tongues, angry that I would subject their children to such coarseness.

Jake rescued the situation by telling another of my time-tested unqualified howlers . . .

This anecdote would be out of place, without import, in any piece that did get written. Fortunately, in this one that didn't, it can be related. And if you insist on searching out a moral, be content with this: never tell your best jokes to that man named Jake.

SO we fished and drank and ate and lusted after the chambermaids, and sometimes the manager would spy us and come asking questions. These had the patina of friendliness, but I knew he was probing, seeing if anything I said sounded even remotely like something that might show up in an article. "This is a great place," I enthused. "This is heaven on earth. Hey," I said, "what do you think of that as a title? 'Heaven on Earth.' "

"It's better than 'The Order of Ideas' or whatever that was."

" 'Heaven on Earth.' Or perhaps—" here comes pompous windbag again, overeager to impress "—'An Angler's Valhalla.' " Try saying that aloud; see if it doesn't sound like mindless gibberish.

One evening we returned and encountered those two salesmen, Ted and Todd, at an open bar. There was something different about them. Ted's eyes radiated a blissful detachment, as though he'd just awoken from an erotic dream or something. And Todd, good buddy Todd, bristled with excitement and kept the barman hopping. Jake and I regarded the pair for a moment and then asked, "What's up?"

Ted's words were long and lazy. "I caught my tyee."

A *tyee* is what they call a salmon that has crossed the twenty-five-pound mark, and catching one is a lifetime achievement. Mind you, you will find people to dispute this. You will find purists—not surprisingly, at the Tyee Club on Vancouver Island—who will tell you that the only legitimate achievement in this regard is to catch a twenty-five-plus salmon *with a fly* and *from a rowboat*. But we didn't want to diminish Ted's radiance, so we shook his hand and got him drinks.

And so to bed, and I suppose I could mention in this piece that never got written that the rooms were first-rate, the beds welcoming and spacious. As I fell asleep on our last night there, I thought maybe I could peddle some little puff piece to, I don't know, *Better Hotels and Motels*, but I suspected there wasn't any such magazine.

I WILL vault ahead in time now, by half a year or so. I am working at my desk, composing a novel, easily squelching the low-level guilt I harbour at having not kept up my part of the bargain with the folks at Tsunami Lodge. I have rationalizations aplenty, chief among them the fact that I could never find the right angle.

Anyway, the phone rings and it's Jake the Joke Thief calling from his home in Manitoba. "Hey, buddy," he says, "did you see the papers today? Tsunami Lodge is all over the front page."

"Really?"

"Yeah. Turns out it's the centre of some big international drug ring."

Jake tells me what the papers report, and we extrapolate from what we had witnessed. Things begin to make sense: a plane lands from Mexico, laden with fishing gear and men in dungarees. They claim they are off angling, and the hidden cargo of narcotics is unsuspected, undetected.

"Shows what kind of investigative journalists *we* are," says Jake.

Well, true. But I was grateful to be let off the hook, because I didn't feel any compunction to play fair with drug dealers. (I can be very sanctimonious when it suits my needs.) And so "The Idea of Order at Tsunami Lodge" remains unwritten.

CAR RIDES

VAGUE coffee, strong thoughts
        I lean my head against the cool
but very hard
glass of the passenger's window
and watch crows pump themselves
up & down
on the soft shoulder

someone in the car is laughing
because the early morning is a good time
to laugh
even a chuckle has tombstone-tumbling
resonance at dawn
that's why someone in the car is laughing
and it may even be me

PICKEREL, PLEASE

PICKEREL fishing is a sport little understood and appreciated, even by those who practise it. Many people go pickerel fishing by default, conspicuously not indulging in the singular pursuit of another species. All other forms of fishing require specialized gear and tactics. Trout fishers wear customized photojournalist vests and silly hats. Bassers drive sleek boats with outboard motors the size of city brownstones. Muskie-men (I have been assiduously trying for gender equality, but the phrase "muskie-men" has too nice a ring to eschew; besides I don't know that I've ever met a muskie-woman) have inflated biceps on their casting arms. Catfish catchers, well, their sport verges on the diabolical, seeing as they labour over huge cauldrons, brewing up matter vile, which they fix to silver hooks and offer up as bait under the spell of the moon.

Pickerel fishers, for the most part, sit quietly in modestly sized and modestly powered boats, waiting.

Oh, certainly, I have heard of—even indulged in—pickerel fishing of a different character. I have, for example, dragged a crankbait through the headwaters of a river in Arkansas, and what's more, I've done that in the middle of the night. And I have often trolled for pickerel, which is similar to sitting quietly in a boat and waiting except for a small *putt-putt-putt-putt* that fills the air. I have back-trolled (*putt-putt-ptui-silence*), and I have aggressively bucked into the current, trying to hold on to a spot in the middle of the Winnipeg River. So I know that one can actively hunt pickerel.

But mostly I, and other pickerel pursuers, sit in a boat and wait.

There is no problem with that except when I am asked to wax poetical about my sport. Indeed, the very word *sport* is a little difficult to apply to the act of sitting in a boat and waiting. *Pastime* springs to mind, doesn't it? Well, fine, let's start there, because the passage of time is one of the attractions of pickerel fishing. For one thing, pickerel fishing is best done at those magical transitional times, as day fades into night or (if you're up for it) as night blossoms into day. Pickerel possess opaque eyes, giving them a look of eldritch blindness, like that elderly Chinese gentleman who extends his palm and says, "Pluck the stone from my palm, Grasshopper." I realize I spent too long on that last simile, but I wanted to emphasize the mystic quality of pickerel eyes, I wanted to distance myself from the rather dismissive "wall-eyed" description that our brothers and sisters to the south rather disdainfully use to name the species. Anyway, because of those eyes, the pickerel's feeding instincts seem to be triggered by a change of light, making dusk and dawn statistically more successful. (Or you could do what some of my muddle-headed friends and I do, knowing about this "change of light" thing: we fish in the middle of the afternoon but pull our sunglasses on and off our faces.)

Beyond the fact that the passage of time itself is rather magical, it is altered by the act of pickerel fishing, which is to say, waiting. Anglers are said to be patient folk, but many know this to be untrue. Anglers are extremely impatient people—they are simply willing to wait *one more minute*. And then just one *more* minute. A succession of such minutes, each distinct and waited out breathlessly, gives a sharply etched brilliance to a morning or an evening spent on the water. That's one of the reasons I go pickerel fishing.

Another consideration is the place where the waiting is to be done. One doesn't simply motor out to the middle of a lake or river and drop anchor. No, no, one spends quite a long time staring at a body of water and its surroundings, squinting into the distance and nodding judiciously. Then one motors out to the middle and drops anchor. Of course, one can get cagey, finding a spot where the body of water narrows. One can use a graph to find a ledge or a sunken island. But pickerel, being a schooling and nomadic fish, are as likely to be one place, wherever that may be, as anywhere else. So, even though the decision may be, in a grand cosmic sense, somewhat arbitrary, at least a decision is being made. The environs, the land and water, are being looked at and admired. That's another reason I go pickerel fishing.

Some people claim that pickerel are rather listless fighters, almost fatalistic, but I can assure you that a three-pound pickerel fights considerably harder than a half-pound trout, a creature that trout fishermen catch more often than they'd like you to think. But even if that slight is deserved, it doesn't matter, because as I've already mentioned, the act of pickerel fishing transforms the very way the angler perceives both time and space.

But if you'd like a less highfalutin reason for my indulging in the sport/pastime, let me mention this: pickerel taste good.

A LITTLE PLACE I KNOW

WHEN my friends and I leave on our fishing expeditions from our home base of Wolverine Lodge, we travel various distances, all of them relatively long: a mile or two upriver, sometimes to the very headwaters. We favour a place we call Third Narrows. (This is the third narrows counting upriver from the Lodge, a huge and hulking construct that sits on the lower branch of central Ontario's Magnetawan River: I guess for other residents of the area they might be Second or Fourth Narrows.) Third Narrows is a clean and bleak place where the river is squeezed together by dark rock. A cottage sits nearby, but there is rarely anybody there. Very occasionally a woman will emerge, wearing a floral muumuu and sipping a cocktail. Usually the world is hushed, except for five men sitting in a boat, pondering the world's mysteries, chief among which is *where are all the fish?*

Mind you, lunkers have been hauled out of the Third Narrows' depths. None by yours truly, but I have been net man on a couple, so I know they're there. The Narrows functions as a kind of turnstile the fish must pass through if they want to go to the amusement park. If one is lucky enough to be sitting on top when they do, well, one is in with a shot, which is why we fish there.

That is why *we* fish there, but *I* don't. What I mean is that fishing is not always a group activity. As Isaak Walton said, fishing is a contemplative pursuit. When I'm in a contemplative mood—it does happen, albeit rarely—I go to the Diner.

I don't know who first dubbed it the Diner, but I know upon publication of this piece that I am going to receive at least nine differing accounts. All these people will claim authorship, which might seem odd. It's not that clever a name, after all, except when you consider how our other fishing spots are named: besides the aforementioned Third Narrows, we have come up with such designations as Second Bay, Sunken Island, Big Tree and so forth. There's a place that we've dubbed the Secret Spot, and that's halfway interesting because there's nothing secret about it. But only the Diner has a kind of evocative whimsy.

Not that the name lacks precision: the Diner is a place where fish drop by to eat. They don't stay long, they don't have a substantial meal, they leave a small tip and move along. But the point is, everyone eventually drops by.

The Diner is a large bite taken out of the shoreline. On either side there are rock faces that slide into the river, but the bite is deep enough that it gets into the mucky tenderness of the forest. There's a bed of lilies, which serves, I believe, as a canopy for bass. (As I say, this is more a matter of belief, of *faith,* than of proven knowledge.) A long time ago, when I first fished there, there was a dead tree lying to one side, and a pike often lurked underneath. (Never a very big pike; this tree seemed to serve as a training ground for teenagers, voracious and skinny things that weighed somewhere between two and three pounds.) But time has gradually melted the tree, and now there is just a kind of ghost tree remaining.

Pike still happen by, but they aren't regulars at the Diner. Indeed, the pike are there for the same reason I am: because other fish are innocently having pie and coffee, chatting about the weather. I recall fishing at the Diner one day, tossing my bait between the lily pads and the ghost tree. (This is where I usually toss my bait. If I were a better angler, I suppose I might toss my bait either *at* the lily pads or *at* the ghost tree, but as it is, I toss my bait somewhere in between.) *Bang-zum,* my lure was gone. Experienced anglers recognize *bang-zum* as the official sensation of a large pike attack when one is using light tackle. *Bang* is the hit, *zum* the terminal tackle being razored away. I retied a jig, and threw it between the pads and the ghost tree. *Bang-zum.* I fished around in my tackle box until I found a wire leader and tied it on quickly. I hesitated before tossing my bait this time, worrying momentarily that I'd tied my knot a little *too* quickly. But I shrugged and threw it in. *Bang,* no *zum;* rather a *zing* as the pike started pulling line from the reel. This was one big fish. How big I can't say because, of course, my knot was no good. There did eventually come a *ping,* and I reeled in and saw the little curlicue at the end of my line that says, "You idiot. Can't you even tie a simple knot?" So while the Diner is usually a place of pleasantness and smallish adventures, it is also deep and dark, and fearsome creatures lurk there. One's knots must always be tested.

When I first went north to the Lodge, I was in my early twenties. Eight of my friends—in effect, eight friend "units," if you will, some bachelors, others already married, only one with children—had pooled their resources and purchased an old fishing lodge. They called it Wolverine Lodge because that name was already there, foot-high letters surmounting the entrance to the front porch. Wolverine Lodge had, has, fourteen bedrooms, two separate cottages (only one of which has been reclaimed from destitution) and a dusty, faded stateliness. The dining room is one hundred feet in length, although the tables are usually pushed more comfortably into one corner, and in that crowded space we sit and eat communally.

Although I was not one of the original purchasers, I have been accepted as a kind of secondary owner, which means that I am responsible, with the others, for financing the maintenance and upkeep. In return, they don't object to my presence there. Indeed, the other Lodgites smile pleasantly upon my arrival and ask how my time in the city has been.

I couldn't have been one of the original owners because, back in my early twenties, I had no money, thanks to the fact that, like many people of that age, I was a bit intemperate in my personal habits. Looking back, I realize I was in desperate need of a hobby.

No, that's not precisely true: I was in desperate need of something
to be passionate about, although that's the sort of desperation that
friends and family find a little worrisome, so I couched it as a need
for a hobby. When I first arrived at the Lodge, half-drunk (an
improvement over my more usual state, bombed), someone stuck
a fishing rod in my hand. We climbed into one of the grey boats
and motored across the river, to the Diner.

They took me to the Diner because the Diner is a good place
to take neophytes. It's easy to catch *something* there. With a piece
of worm and a little hook, for example, it's extremely easy to catch
a sunfish. After catching a sunfish, Wolverine Lodgites say, "Always a pleasure." By this we allude to the fishes' behaviour of turning rapid circles, establishing centrifugal force, making them feel
much larger than they actually are.

That was the first fish I caught, a sunfish. Oh, I suppose I had
angled as a youngster, sharing a rowboat with my father and brothers, but I was never enthusiastic and quite possibly never took anything from the water. I sat there, bored and restless. I spent a lot of
time wondering whether or not I could receive television transmissions within my own body, if I could somehow project images
upon my closed eyelids. And, truth to tell, I was a bit bored at the
Diner that first evening. My borrowed rod was one of those cob-
webbed, rusty contraptions that cottages and camps yield up, and
I dropped my bait into the water without expectation of success. I
was therefore somewhat surprised, startled even, to have the line

tighten, to see the rod tip jerk erratically. It was this sensation—of being attached to life, frantic and unrelenting—that whetted my appetite for fishing.

I organized another expedition for the following morning. Not the following *early* morning, mind you; it would be some time before I discovered angling's dark and dirty secret, that it is best done at times when sensible people are asleep. No, I forced my friends to take me out sometime after breakfast and hangover dissipation, around 11:30. Not, as you know, the best time to go. The sun is too much for most of the species, so they vanish into the cooler depths. This, then, is when I first encountered rock bass.

The "scourge," that's what we Lodgites call rock bass. Name-calling is as far as our dislike typically manifests itself. I have heard of some anglers wantonly doing damage to the greedy little fish—bouncing them off the motor transom in the process of returning them to the water—but we do our best to be nice. I believe the act of angling, which situates the angler more securely in the food chain, fosters a greater respect for the whole system, even for the little red-eyed scourge. (My own idiosyncratic manner of banishing disdain is to refer to some of these less sporty fish by more sporty names: rock bass become "black bass," sunfish are the more reputable "bluegill," and the tiny perch is, in my terminology, a "tiger fish.")

I had become a keen angler in the space of a few hours, but, of course, I was an unskilled one. I knew nothing of hook sets, so when the first nibbles came that late morning, I didn't react well.

Oh, I had fun—I flushed and horripilated, I grinned and chuckled—but I allowed the little fish too long a nosh, and by the time I brought it up, the hook was well down its gorge. The ensuing operation did not go well, and as I tossed the corpse of an innocent "black bass" into the nearby greenery, I said to myself, "Well, Paul, if you're going to do this fishing thing, you'd better learn to do it a lot better than that." And the Diner was my school.

My friends were my actual teachers. They taught me all the basic stuff: how to flip the bail, let the bait down until the line goes slack, crank the handle a time or two to raise the jig, then bounce it slowly back toward the boat. My friends also taught me how to set the hook, although some of them have rather peculiar notions and habits. Professor Bill, for example—the only Lodge member whose affection for the Diner rivals my own—sometimes likes to balance his rod on one finger, and then keeps the other hand poised above the butt, ready to slap down and imbed the hook. This can be very effective. On more than one occasion Professor Bill has slapped down with such force that a poor little black bass has flown up into the air and described a beautiful rainbow as it returns to the water on the other side of the boat. So my friends taught me presentation and delivery, if you will, which are undeniably important. I had to teach myself about the stuff in between.

First there is the waiting. It is commonly understood that fishing requires patience. This is commonly understood, of course, by people who don't fish. Anglers know that fishing requires *impatience*.

There may be stillness involved—fish don't like people banging about in boats—but there is much internal fidgeting. *Am I sitting in the right place?* the angler wonders. *Should I have gone with the pink jighead, or was that just errant foolishness?* There are decisions and observations to be made, much theorizing to be done. There is that most human of activities—sticking around to see what will happen next. One moment follows another, then another. Chopping up time like so makes it seem more precious; one is like the king in his counting house, and the treasure seems limitless.

And what are we waiting for? Not a fish, precisely, but a nibble, the light tapping as the fish mouths the bait, the announcement of piscatorial life. That is the thrill of the thing to me, just as a Lothario is more excited by a glance and a half-smile than the actual sexual encounter—all right, all right, poor example. But my memories of the Diner are not as much of fish being caught-boated or released—as of having my reverie interrupted by a tug on the line.

My favourite tugs, the ones that give me the most goose bumps per square inch of flesh, are rendered by bass. There are both smallmouth and largemouth in the river, and although the Diner is a likelier habitat for the former, I have pulled up largemouth. I recall one day when there was a bigger-than-average boatload of anglers over at the Diner, six mates in an aluminum boat. "Look," someone whispered, pointing with a rod tip. In the clear shallow between the lily pads and the shore was a largemouth, a huge brutish thing on the prowl. There was a moment's silence as we all marvelled at its size; this fish would have dwarfed the mounts on the Lodge wall, dusty artifacts left behind by the former occupants. But our moment of reverential awe was shattered when six lures (aimed with uncommon accuracy) landed on top of the fish. The bass disappeared so suddenly that it seemed like sorcery.

As I say, smallmouth bass are more common at the Diner. They're certainly not always there, or even there with any regularity. If I may extend the Diner analogy, bass are kind of like city work crews; they show up to eat at odd hours, operating on some schedule known only to the bureaucrats at lofty levels. Actually, the analogy works fairly well, because the fish also tend to be well-muscled, and they don't mind a fight.

Over the years I have caught many species at the Diner, including some unexpected pickerel. I say *unexpected* pickerel because, as my keenness for the pursuit increased, I spent my off-hours voraciously reading angling magazines and how-to books. So I knew about pickerel, how they feed at night on flats, how they are a schooling fish. I'd studied pickerel with the intensity of a Talmudic scholar, so I knew it was strange to pick up a cruising singleton over at the Diner. But from this I learnt my single greatest lesson: fish don't read those books and magazines.

Once I'd accepted that, I was open to all manner of experience. I remember on one occasion fishing at dawn. (Let me come clean: I met this dawn from the other end, driving all night in my rusted-out Mustang, and hopping into a boat just as the moon was starting to crack.) I went over to the Diner and began to fish. I was embroiled in a very ugly love affair at the time, but it's impossible to both fish *and* be embroiled in a very ugly love affair. That is both the great gift and the great toll of fishing—it demands that you commit to it and it alone. But there soon arrived a kind of poetic coincidence; I caught a very ugly fish. I am not sure to this day what sort of fish it was. My best guess is that it was a ling. At any rate, as I've told the story over time, I've settled on ling. People have nodded, and one or two have told me that ling are good to eat, which just goes to show, it takes all kinds. I couldn't even bring myself to touch it. I cut the line and it went back to the Diner and I haven't seen it or its ilk since.

Eventually I progressed from an unskilled angler to a poorly schooled one. It was then my turn to take neophytes over to the Diner. During my late twenties and early thirties, I took a variety of female friends over there. If I may broach this subject—and given that I'm wielding the pen here, there's no stopping me—let me say that, being a halfway evolved fellow, it does not bother me that some women are better anglers than I. It does, however, rankle that virtually *all* women are better anglers than I. I have various theories as to why this might be. For one thing, they typically haven't spent as much time reading angling magazines and how-to books, so aren't as educated, which gives them a real advantage. Women tend to fish where they shouldn't, and they usually catch the fish that shouldn't even be there. Also, women are patient. Not just still, as men can train themselves to be, but very patient. They will hold their bait in the water long enough for fish to find it, unlike many of my own gender, who constantly reel up to check on the situation or to reposition the terminal tackle. My final theory is a bit less tangible, maybe less credible. But being more sensitive in most regards, I believe women are on to it just a fraction of a second earlier than men when a fish comes poking along down in the deep darkness. And men lose a lot of fish in a fraction of a second. As I say, this theory is certainly up for debate, but I believe women are just more attuned to, well, life.

One of these female friends—the last of the succession, I hasten to point out—became the mother of my two children. The Diner is the only place to take kids. I've tried taking them on more "serious" fishing expeditions. I've taken them to Third Narrows and watched their little eyes glaze over. "No," I tell them. "It's impossible. You can't receive television transmissions, not even now that the sky is filled with communication satellites." Even at the Diner I contrive to have snacks, cold drinks and, if possible, casino games on board for diversion. But the regulars at the Diner—I am referring to the fish now—show up often enough to keep the kids amused. And I hope that when they grow up—I'm referring to the kids now—they will take their own children there.

My wife and I go there, from time to time. We are trying to work things out, but even when our marriage lay in ruins we still somehow found time to go to the Diner. On a perfectly still summer's evening, the flat surface of the water makes it the best place to reflect on the bumps and dents on time's road. We don't talk much, but something about the Diner takes the air out of the silence.

Still, I mostly go to the Diner on my own, especially when the vagaries of life are weighing on my mind. As I mentioned, it is impossible to fish and still have the vagaries of life weighing on one's mind. That's why I'm a fisherman.

THE Diner has changed a little this season. The ghost tree is even ghostlier, although, of course, I still get hung up in phantom lumber. The water level is low, so little space remains between the lily pads and the shoreline, certainly not enough to allow the passage of a lunker largemouth. But it's still the Diner, a place where fish and people congregate, a place that is very much full of life.

I still haven't told you the very best thing about the Diner, which is its proximity to Wolverine Lodge. It is the perfect distance away from the building. When twilight comes and dinnertime nears, a Lodge member will come to stand upon the lawn. He or she will cup hands and bellow for me to come eat. The Diner is near enough to the Lodge that I can, if I choose, look up, smile and wave, and head for home. But the Diner is also far enough away that I can ignore this call without hurting any feelings. And then I can remain praying over my rod, waiting for a nibble.

MY FAVOURITE DAY
OF THE WEEK

TOMORROW I'll be bilious,
  Full of battery acid,
Because I've stayed up
Too late squeezing whiskey glasses.

Tomorrow I must rise to meet dawn:
I am going fishing.
So I really should sleep
But I'm too excited for sleep
Because tomorrow I will rise and kiss dawn.

I am going fishing.

Acknowledgements

THE author would like to thank Rob Sanders, Barbara Pulling and Dorothy Bennie for their help in pulling together this manuscript; Patrick Walsh, James Little, David Zimmer and Bart Robinson for help on the individual pieces; and Jake MacDonald, Chris Conway, Peter Oliva, Gordon Deval, Rick Matusiak and Paul Kennedy for their help with the hard work, the actual fishing.